Ja

Romans 12:12

Love,

Lynda Strahorn

— WE —
LAUGHED
— 'TIL WE —
CRIED

LYNDA STRAHORN

*LIVING,
LOVING
AND
LAUGHING
WITH
ALS*

WE
LAUGHED
'TIL WE
CRIED

TATE PUBLISHING
AND ENTERPRISES, LLC

Published by Tate Publishing & Enterprises, LLC
127 E. Trade Center Terrace | Mustang, Oklahoma 73064 USA
1.888.361.9473 | www.tatepublishing.com

Tate Publishing is committed to excellence in the publishing industry. The company reflects the philosophy established by the founders, based on Psalm 68:11,
"The Lord gave the word and great was the company of those who published it."

Published in the United States of America

ISBN: 978-1-68333-600-6
1. Family & Relationships / Death, Grief, Bereavement
2. Biography & Autobiography / Personal Memoirs
16.05.03

Dedicated to my soul mate, my best friend,
my biggest fan, and my angel, Don.

Acknowledgments

I know the seeds that were planted for this book was the Lord's prompting. This is never something I would have ever thought I could do, but I'm finding out the Lord has a lot of things in store for me that I never thought possible. Don insisted from the very beginning that the Lord would use him somehow when he was diagnosed with ALS. I know that is true now, and I also know He is not done with me or our family yet. How this book came into being is proof of that, and I'd like to thank those who helped make this possible as well as those who played a role in the story these pages hold.

First, I want to say thank you, Lord Jesus, for using me.

With that, I am forever grateful for the following people:

Our children: Ryan, Jennifer, Jaclyn, and Jonathan, who have been our greatest blessing. We always knew this, but the way you all stepped in and showed unconditional love for your dad and me while you were also hurting showed such strength and love. Thank you for *always* being there at a moment's notice with help, laughter, and love. You'll just never know.

Our children's spouses: Terri, Jeremy, Clint, and Brandy. Thank you for never questioning a call in the middle of the night when we needed help, and thank you for loving our children and supporting them through these seven years.

Our grandchildren: Carlie, Harison, Carter, Hutch, Cooper, Emily, Avery, and Olivia. Joy, pure joy is what you bring us—laughter and love in all the times we need it the most. You made your Papa's last years so amazing.

Our parents: Jack and DewAnn, and Claudette and Lynn. The love and support you showed as this weighed so heavy on your own hearts kept me going, and still does. You all taught us so much about marriage and how to put others first. Thank you.

My sisters, Donna and Camille, thank you for easing Don's mind by telling him you would make sure that you would help me through the foggy time and teach me how to take care of myself. You've always been there.

Don's brother, Tom, thank you for your support and for calling Don and always asking for his opinion when he wasn't able to be there at work; it meant the world to him.

All our family and friends. What would we have done without you? We just couldn't have made it without all your love and support, from the beginning to the end. You were always there in so many different ways.

Team Strahorn. You are truly a group of treasured and diverse friends. You are our children's friends, high school friends, church friends, and community friends, and you came through for us in ways I could have never imagined. From casseroles to bathroom remodels to sending us on family trips that gave us memories we will always have, you were there to take care of us in ways that just blew me away.

Our Meadowood Church family. Don and I had no idea when we joined this church thirty-five years ago what a blessing it would become to us. We raised our children in this church and baptized them there, and three of them were married there. Some of our biggest life-changing moments were spent within the walls of this church, including Don's memorial service. You all are the rock when the winds beat against us.

Allen and Debbie Clark, you have loved us in so many different ways—some of them Don knew about and some he didn't. I can never thank you enough.

Roy and Dee Manley, you amazed Don and me each month with your loving and giving spirit from the very beginning of Don's battle till this very day. Your generosity will never be forgotten by our family.

Kathy McCarley, our hospice nurse. You became both family and friend. You listened and loved us as your own, and you will never know how much you meant to us.

Don's doctors. You were honest and truthful, professional and caring. You truly blessed us with first-class care.

Our community. We have been a part of this community all our lives. Thanks for all the support.

Richard Tate of Tate Publishing. The Lord put you next to me while judging a pageant on purpose. When you told me I needed to write a book, you made it happen, even when I told you that there was no way I could do it. Thank you for talking me into listening to you and having a vision for what this book could be.

Cassandra "Kasey" Woody. You've made it happen! When I said I couldn't do this because I wasn't a writer, I was told I may not be a writer but I'm an author. I understand the difference now. You, young lady, are a *writer*. Without you, this would have never worked. You have taken the CarePages and video, listened to me, and taken my poorly written stories and gotten into my brain someway and made this readable! I couldn't be more pleased with you as my writer!

Don. Thank you for picking me to be your wife. Don, I'm telling our story—our story. It is a love story, and I don't like the way it ended, but I am so thankful the Lord chose me to care for you.

What a privilege. Don, you would have loved everything about this book and how it all came about. Who knows? Maybe you had something to do with it! I love you with all my heart and forever. And I'll see you soon.

CONTENTS

Foreword

To me, courageous behavior and character equals Bravery. Complete trust and a strong belief in God based on spiritual guidance rather than proof means faith. And an intense feeling of deep affection stands for love. As you experience each chapter that takes you down this unfair but amazing journey of one family's battle with the disease of ALS, narrated through the eyes of Lynda and Don Strahorn, you will no doubt see all these traits. I am fortunate to have witnessed firsthand what true bravery, faith, and love really mean. Why? Because Don Strahorn embraced and shared bravery, faith, and love with me most of his life, especially during the last years of his time on earth. He showed me what these abstract terms look like while facing unprecedented odds.

My wife, Sandy, and I discussed our childhood days quite often. She always reminds me how lucky I am to still have childhood friends. She was what they called a "military brat" and moved often, leaving many close relationships behind. I agree that I have been blessed, but with those bonds come a price. The price we pay for such special and long-lasting bonds is losing the person you have shared so much with prematurely. We all know that death is a part of life, but when it comes unexpectedly and far before it should, a different kind of void is left in its wake.

I've known Don since the 1960s. We became best friends as kids, and the friendship that started between two awkward pre-teens lasted for decades until ALS took my best friend. I may have lost Don physically, but he has hardly left me or anyone else he touched. I tell everyone—and I mean everyone—about the character Don displayed throughout his life, and most certainly the final seven years after his diagnosis. Don's deep relationship with God was a true testimony. He faced a terminal illness with grace I could have never imagined. But Don always did have an air of maturity and an outlook like no one I knew, even as a young man. He married the love of his life, Lynda, right out of high school. He worked tirelessly, transforming an idea into a successful landscaping business. These alone are premiere accomplishments, but the most impressive contribution Don made was the four beautiful children he and Lynda raised, who continue to resonate the Strahorn legacy.

Don was the guy we all wanted to be: happy, respected, loved, and God-fearing. Don and I had always been close, but ALS took our friendship to a new level. He taught me in a short period of time how to eloquently prepare and conquer death by living a life full of appreciation. In our fast-paced world, we take for granted all the things ALS strips from its victims: walking, speaking, independence, and eventually life itself. I don't know how I would react to my impending death, but I now have a reference of how I should act thanks to Don Strahorn. Through all the losses he experienced, he stayed focused on what he still had. He thanked God for the blessings instead of asking "Why me?"

Lynda too was an inspiration to see the last seven years of her husband's life. She dedicated the last several years of her life serving the man she loved. People don't realize that the simplest tasks become overwhelming when dealing with ALS. Lynda helped Don with all those not-so-simple-anymore tasks. She honored her vows to Don and to God, through "sickness and in health 'till death do us part." She too is a true hero in this life-and-death story.

God knows the answers and provides us opportunity during despair. Don took death and showed every person he touched that he lived his life the same before and after ALS. It was a logical choice for a man who always did the right thing in life. As I close, I want to thank the Strahorn family for sharing this experience and helping me and so many others understand that actions rooted in the honor of God will yield the best outcome, even when our minds cannot comprehend how or why that can happen.

I got to say good-bye to my friend Don Strahorn the day he died. He was surrounded by family, and they were gracious enough to allow me into the bedroom as time dwindled away. I held Don's hand, kissed him on the forehead, and told him I loved him. Don, who was semi-conscious, opened his eyes and whispered, "I love you too!" A few hours later, God welcomed Don into heaven and released him from ALS.

God bless Don and Lynda Strahorn!

You will never be forgotten my dear friend.

With brotherly love,

Brandon Clabes
Chief of Police
Midwest City, Oklahoma

PREFACE

About ALS

My husband, Don, was diagnosed with ALS in March 2007. When he was first diagnosed, we had so many questions. The problem with ALS is that there really is no answer to the questions you have in the beginning because it affects each person differently. My family and I witnessed this firsthand in so many ways over the seven years Don battled the disease. From the patients we saw in the waiting room at Don's many doctor's appointments to the people we met in support groups and at ALS awareness events, we learned very quickly that ALS is not a cut-and-dried disease. Whether it starts in your foot or with your speech, whether it is a quick or long battle, whether you have little or a lot of support, no two people diagnosed with ALS have the same experience. That's what makes it so frustrating and so difficult to deal with and prepare for. There is no cure for ALS, and to this day, doctors still have not figured out what causes it.

In Don's case, it seemed to be so random. No one in his family had ever had it. And Don was a completely healthy man his entire life until ALS set in. It's a tricky disease to say the least. That is why I decided to write this book: to shed some light on such an obscure disease. See, when Don was first diagnosed, I knew as much about ALS as I did rocket science. I had no idea what to expect or what we were in for. Because ALS is so different for patients, there is no way I could know completely, but as Don and I started doing some digging to find any kind of answers we could, I realized that there isn't much written about the disease or how to deal with it when a loved one is diagnosed. This book is my small attempt to remedy that. Although the only guarantee you get with an ALS diagnosis is that there are no guarantees except death, I hope that this book can answer some of the bigger questions that I couldn't find answers to when I went looking for them. I also hope that it can bring a little bit of peace in the midst of a life-altering event while also helping to prepare for what is to come. Mostly, I want to let people see how just one family dealt with the bittersweet moments of the disease—how we chose to laugh whenever we could, but also cried when we needed to—so that everyone dealing with it will know they are not alone.

1

Something Is Off

April 2007 of us and the kids right after diagnosis:
Ryan, Jennifer, Me, Don, Jaclyn and Jonathan

"If you are watching this, it means that something has happened to me. They have probably already taken my body by now for evidence." Don has a sly grin on his face as he looks into the camera. "Is it on? Can you hear me?" he shouts, obviously amused with himself.

"You dork," our daughter Jaclyn giggles in the background.

"Well, I had to say something," Don quips back. He is making his farewell to us. This is the way he decided to start it off. He is in his wheelchair by this point. His speech is impeccable considering how far along the disease is, but when he lifts his left hand to wipe tears every now and again, you can see the atrophy in his thin wrists.

"You can edit this," Don says after a long pause as he tries to gather himself.

"Yeah," Jaclyn replies from behind the camera. Fifteen minutes into the recording, Don starts over, another mischievous grin planted on his face: "If you are seeing this, it means something has happened to me." The fifteen minutes that preceded this second take were filled with laughter and tears. He is saying good-bye to his family—to *our* family.

"Your mom wanted me to do this so she could remember my voice," he explains to my daughter. "I don't know why though. She has Emily."

Emily is our granddaughter, and she has so much character I don't know where she fits all of it. Don lifts his arm and buries his mouth in the crook of it. He starts to talk; his voice is muffled by his arm.

"Momma, can you help me? Momma, can you come in here? Momma, can you wipe my butt?" he says into his arm. He is mimicking Emily mimicking him. She had taken to imitating her Papa by burying her mouth into her arm, the way Don does in the video, and yelling out like Don did across the house to get my attention when he needed anything. Her Papa found the whole thing hilarious. Don lowers his arm from his mouth and smiles. "She always has Emily," he says again, drifting off into his thoughts.

The video goes on for about forty-eight minutes. In it, Don gives advice, cracks jokes, chokes on his words now and again, and gives me a drink order over the phone when I call and interrupt the process. "Hello," he says as he picks up the phone. "We're live and streaming. Is there anything you want me to say about you? I already did the fruits of the spirit and told them you were lacking in the gentleness area." I'm so loud you can nearly hear me on the recording through the phone. Don mentions my loudness on more than one occasion in this recording. In true Lynda fashion, I scold him for his little jab and tell him if he wants a drink order, he'd better tell me. He asks for a Dr. Pepper and says he'll see me soon.

After he hangs up, Don lists off some quotes he wants the kids to remember. "You can't fix stupid," he says with a smirk. His words of wisdom include things like "Always give a courtesy flush." That was Don. He never, ever lost that sense of humor. The video ends when he hears my car pull into the drive.

"I gotta get outta here," he says to the camera. "I'll see y'all. I love you."

21

In December 2006, Don and I and took our daughter and son-in-law to the Chesapeake arena in downtown Oklahoma City to see the Trans-Siberian Orchestra Christmas concert. The four of us rode together. Don drove, as always. He claimed my driving was somewhat questionable. I thought he was full of it, but I let him drive anyway. It gave me more time to chat with my daughter, and it kept Don from becoming the world's worst backseat driver. It was also pretty chilly that day, so I was happy to have Don drop us off at the entrance so I wouldn't have to walk the mile in heels from the parking place.

"We'll meet you at the seats," I told him as I hopped out of the car.

"Be there in a minute," he said.

The three of us got inside and settled in. The concert was about to start. I hoped that Don would find a place easily so he didn't miss the beginning. It took him a bit longer than I expected. *Probably can't find a space*, I thought as I glanced back at the door every minute to see if he had made it in. Finally, right as the concert was getting ready to start, Don made it to our seats.

"I almost didn't make it here," he whispered as he took his seat beside me.

"What?" I asked. "What do you mean?" My first thought was someone must've tried to mug him in the parking lot. I have a wild imagination.

As the lights dimmed across the arena, he whispered back, "I don't know what's going on. My right foot just wasn't working right. It just kept getting weaker as I was walking."

Don shrugged as the music began, and we turned our attention to the flashing lights and booming music in front of us. We sat and watched the concert, and I didn't think much more about how long it took him to get there. To tell you the truth, I was just relieved that he hadn't been mugged. Don had been limping a little bit since about May of that year. We hadn't thought anything about it though. And I didn't think too much about it that night. But the limping didn't go away. And it started to seem like maybe it was something to think about. So in January when I had to go to the doctor for a cold and as I was telling him about how much snot had been coming out of me over the last week, I remembered Don's limping, and I mentioned that too.

"He nearly didn't make it into the concert," I said. "He said his foot just wouldn't cooperate."

"You should have him come in," he told me. "It sounds like a pinched nerve or something. I'll take a look at him and see what I think."

I relayed the message to Don, and eventually, he got around to going to the doctor. He owned a landscaping business and he hated taking time off, so it wasn't easy to convince him to go. He did though, and then he went to see a specialist in February and found out he had something called a *foot drop* in his right foot. We had to see what was causing this foot drop, so next it was more specialists and tests. Don had an MRI, which showed there was no pinched nerve. In March, they sent him to a neurologist where he had an EMG. We were waiting for the results of that.

I was at the church decorating with family and friends. I think I was as excited as the bride-to-be about the upcoming wedding. I was also focused. My sole mission was to make everything beautiful. As I was buzzing around the church placing vases and straightening decorations at the end of pews, Don was at the neurologist's office getting his test results. I wasn't that worried about the tests. I figured it was something small—something that could be fixed with a little operation or some time in a boot. Don, always the one to be prepared, had done some research about his symptoms and mentioned that ALS was coming up.

"Lynda, it says here it could be ALS," he told me as his eyes scanned the computer screen.

I didn't know much about ALS, but it didn't sound good. I asked him, "What is that? It's not good is it?" It wasn't. He explained it to me a bit, and I stopped him. "Well, it isn't that!" I told him, and we went about our business.

The results Don got that day were not hopeful. Something was definitely going on, and the neurologist had a strong suspicion that my husband was in the beginning stages of ALS, also known as Lou Gehrig's disease, also known as a disease with no cure. My daughter was going to be married in less than twenty-four hours, and there Don was, listening to a doctor tell him he probably had a terminal disease. Talk about timing. I remember right where I was when he called after his appointment and told me.

"Lynda, they think it is ALS. They want me to go to Houston to see a doctor who specializes in it."

"What does that mean, Don?" I asked.

"It means we need some more tests, but he's pretty sure," he told me. "But I don't want you saying anything to anyone. Tomorrow is Jennifer's special day, and she doesn't need to hear this right before it."

"You're totally right," I said, trying to sort out my own feelings. I was a jumbled up mess by then. I was about to watch my sweet daughter get married, and I had just heard my husband may have a terminal disease. How do you even begin to make sense of that?

"I'll just talk to Bob about it for now," he told me. Bob Rutherford was our pastor and one of Don's best friends. He was up at the church as well that evening. He would be marrying our daughter the next day so he was there for rehearsals. Don and I met in the hall of the church when he got there. Don's eyes were a little red and puffy. I could tell he had been crying. I felt the burn of tears in my eyes when I saw this.

"We just have to pull it together right now," he said. "This is about Jennifer right now. This is a happy time. We're gonna get through the next few days and make sure that this is one of the happiest moments of her life."

"Okay," I said. "We will."

After we talked, Don went to Bob's office and told him about the diagnosis. They both cried in the privacy of his office. While they were in there crying, we were just outside the door, smiling and laughing as we prepared Jennifer for married life and fussed over whether or not there were too many flowers at the altar. Don left after that, and Bob came and found me. I remember him saying, "I don't know how you, Don, and I are going to get through this tonight," and then we cried. My mom was there and she could tell that something was going on, so I took her aside and told her. A few hours later, rehearsal began, and we all sucked it up. Don and I greeted everyone with smiles. I was talkative as always, and Don was glowing with pride for our daughter. We went on like nothing else was on our minds. We pushed the news aside to make the perfect wedding for our daughter.

That night we went home, and finally we let go. Don and I lay in bed, holding each other and crying. We were both awake when the phone rang at midnight. It was Jen. She too was in tears, but for an entirely different reason. She was having some anxiety about the wedding.

"I need you right now, Mom," she whimpered into the phone. As I listened to her, I sat and stared at Don. He needed me too. I didn't know what to do.

"Go," Don told me. "I'm gonna be fine."

"Are you sure?" I asked.

"She's getting married tomorrow. You go and make her feel better," he insisted. "It's what moms do." So I went, and

I stayed with her until six in the morning. All I could think about was Don all alone. I got home and climbed into bed with him when I finally left my dozing daughter. We both cried some more.

I remember thinking, *How in the world am I going to make it today?* I was going on a couple of hours of sleep and had a pain in my heart I had never felt before. But on the other hand, I also had so much joy; it was my daughter's wedding day.

That day when the *Bridal Chorus* began, I stood for the bride to walk down the aisle and felt a rush of emotions hit me so hard I almost fell over. I looked at her and Don and started to cry. I thought, *Lord, I don't know what's in store, but I want to remember this moment.* Don looked so handsome, and she was just beautiful. I was so thankful for the strong man I had married. Then all the sudden, I remembered Bob. He knew too. He was thinking some of the same things I was. He was watching Don walk his daughter down the aisle, knowing he has this disease. I was all tears, but Bob had to keep it together. He was front and center. I turned to look up at our pastor and saw that he had a pinched expression on his face. I knew he was fighting back the tears. We all were.

We did it. We all made it through. I watched my daughter say "I do" and begin the next phase in her life. I knew that Don and I were starting a new phase in ours as well that day. During the vows, the words "for better or worse, in sickness and health, till death do you part" struck me like they never had before. It was time to make good on those vows; I knew that. But I really had no idea at all what was in store. Mostly though, I didn't think Don could surprise me anymore. He did though. His strength and love and humor through the next seven years just blew me away. I don't know how many people can say this, but we laughed our way through ALS. There were tears shed for sure, but there was so much laughter too. It got so hard that sometimes that was all we could do. Just laugh.

Jennifer and me right before her wedding

Don and me at Jennifer's wedding

Jennifer and Don

Jaclyn and Don at Jaclyn's wedding

2

This Ain't Grey's Anatomy

The day after Jennifer's wedding, we had all the kids come to the house to break the news. Jennifer was on her honeymoon, so we decided to tell her when she returned. I don't know that I've ever done anything more difficult than that. Not only did we have to say it out loud once again but we were also going to have to tell our children. It was our job to protect them from the world, but we were about to deliver the worst news of their lives. There's just no way to prepare them for such a thing. When everyone was present and accounted for, Don started. We were all at the kitchen table, like we had been for countless family dinners in the past. This time would be different from the rest though.

"I've asked you all to come here because Mom and I have something to tell you," Don started. I could see his eyes glazing over and knew that he wasn't going to get through it. "I had to see a specialist about my limp, and he thinks..." Don's voice cracked, so I stepped in. It was time for me to be strong for us now.

"They think your dad might have ALS," I said, relieving Don of the task. "We are going to go to Houston to see a specialist to find out for sure, but the doctor is pretty certain that is what it is."

At that, I held my breath and waited. Jonathan, who is a firefighter and always the one to fix a problem, did exactly as I had expected; he immediately started trying to figure out how he could fix everything. He wanted to know the details and to know what he needed to do to make it easier on us. He wanted to get a second opinion too to make sure that there wasn't some kind of mix-up. And he wanted to know every treatment out there and what kind of research was being done on ALS. Just like his father, Jonathan wanted to be prepared and thought the more he knew, the better chance he had at figuring the problem out. Our other son seemed a bit less taken off guard. He had been bracing himself for the announcement since Don started having tests done. He had developed a bad feeling since Don's limping had gotten worse. Then there was Jaclyn. Jaclyn just broke down into tears. Like me, she wanted to know why—why her daddy? Why this disease? Why?

"I know it's hard, but we aren't going to ask why," Don said when he got himself reeled in. "I know that there is a reason to all this. God is going to use this for good. So we aren't going to ask why. We are going to ask how God will use this for good."

Jennifer got home, and we had to break the news all over again. I think she took the news the hardest. Don reiterated that we would stay positive and look for the way God would use this for His glory. I could hardly believe it. I knew Don was a godly man. I also knew he had an unshakable faith. But that he could stare death right in the face and say "Let's not ask why" even at the very beginning, well, that was something I don't think anyone expects. His faith gave us faith though. Don became an example for me and the kids in every way. He showed us how a person could be strong in the most vulnerable of situations. Most importantly, Don's strength let us see that we could all make it, no matter what happened. It also reminded us that God was in charge and that He had bigger plans than we could see. That's something that is easy to forget when you get news you don't want. Don was helping us to remember. Every day and every smile, Don was helping us to remember. It didn't make what we were dealing with easy by any stretch of the imagination, but it did help us learn to lean on Jesus more than ever. And it gave us peace when we should have felt anything but. Now don't get me wrong; we'd have our times of pain. But it was succeeded and preceded by comfort, and it has always been eclipsed by love. And that love started from the word *go*. I mean, right out of the gates we were swallowed up by it. If we didn't realize how blessed we were before the diagnosis, we most certainly did in the years following it.

"You ready to go, Don?" I called across the house as I lugged a suitcase to the door.

"Ready as I'll ever be," he said as he made one last round to check that everything was in order before we left. Our next stop was Houston, Texas, where Don would be poked and prodded by one of the best ALS specialists in the country. It had been three weeks since the neurologist first dropped the bomb on us. He recommended we go to Houston for the next round of testing. Luckily for us, we had friends there: Rod and Pam. When we asked if they minded last-minute visitors, they were more than happy to have us. I don't think I could ever thank these two enough. I was grateful that they were willing to open their house to us as we started out on the most difficult journey we'd ever endured. But Pam and Rod did much more than offer us a warm bed and a place to shower in the mornings. They were a complete support system the entire time we were there. Rod started and stopped his days for us whenever we needed him. Before we could even ask, he was there, ready and willing to do whatever needed to be done. All the while, Pam opened her beautiful home to us without hesitation and cooked every meal for us. They both prayed with us and loved us every minute we were there. As strange as it is to say, they found a way to make that trip enjoyable. We were getting the worst news of our lives, but at the same time, we were also experiencing so much love that we couldn't help but feel absolutely blessed. It was like Jen's wedding all over again. It was pain and joy all mixed into one weird experience.

While in Houston, we called the kids daily to keep them up to date on what was going on. Most days the news was there was no news. I was becoming quite knowledgeable on medical lingo, however. Halfway through our stay, I was convinced that I could be a doctor, or at the very least play one on *Grey's Anatomy*. I told the kids this when they would ask what we found out.

"How was it today?" Jaclyn would ask.

"It was just like being an extra on *House* or *Grey's Anatomy*," I'd tell her. "I haven't seen a Dr. McDreamy anywhere though. He must be in oncology."

As I moved through what felt like a hospital melodrama, we were showered with thoughts, prayers, and cards from all over the place. Since we first found out, we had people from all over calling, dropping in with meals, and even making donations to help pay bills. Don got more fan mail than Patrick Dempsey. At the end of it all though, we didn't get to walk away from the set and go back to our lives. There was nobody calling for a cut so we could quit playing the family with an ALS diagnosis. At the end of it all, the doctors in Houston confirmed what we hoped and prayed would not be true.

"This is a tricky disease because there is no test to tell you if have ALS, so the testing we've been doing is just ruling out other things. But I am 99 percent sure that it is ALS," the doctor explained. He was wearing his white coat and bow tie, as usual. His voice was calm and comforting, as it had been the entire time. It was terrible news, but I couldn't have asked to receive it from a better doctor. "ALS is sometimes called the nice man's disease, and it seems that it really is."

"Well, it sure got the right man," I replied as I squeezed Don's hand.

"I know," the doctor said with a pitiful look on his face. "I'm so sorry."

He went on to tell us a bunch of stuff Don had already found out doing his own research. The disease is a progressive neurodegenerative disease that affects nerve cells in the brain and the spinal cord. Motor neurons reach from the brain to the spinal cord and from the spinal cord to all the muscles throughout the body. The progressive degeneration of the motor neurons in ALS eventually lead to their death. When the motor neurons die, the brain's ability to initiate and control muscle movement is lost. With voluntary muscle action progressively affected, patients in the later stages of the disease may become totally paralyzed. Yet through it all, for the vast majority of people, their minds remain unaffected.

This news came after a series of tests. There were the two initial EMGs that he did back in Oklahoma, and then in Houston, Don went through MRIs, blood work, and spinal taps. The tests seem to get progressively worse as they went. The EMG was uncomfortable at best and sometimes even painful, depending on where they were testing. For anyone not familiar with an EMG, what they do is stick small needles into the muscles and shock them to see how they respond. They put needles in Don's tongue, neck, legs, arms, anywhere there's a muscle, really. He was like a life-size voodoo doll. In Oklahoma, I hadn't been present when they did the tests, but in Houston I was able to watch. I didn't know how I'd handle it at first. I was actually a little surprised at my own reaction. I think the tech was too! Rather than shielding my eyes as they stuck him with needles, I was right up in the mix.

"So where will you put the next one?" I asked as the tech pulled a needle from Don's arm.

"In another muscle in the arm," he told me.

"How much will you shock him this time?" I asked. I was like a kid watching a science experiment.

After the last shock, the tech told us that we were all done with the EMG. Don had a question of his own at that. "Since I'm all done, you can go ahead and hook my wife up to the machine and give her a little sample, since she thinks it's so interesting."

"No thanks!" I declined the offer. I may have liked to watch, but I was fine remaining a spectator. When we were riding home from the hospital after the day I had sat in on an EMG, I had to confess something to my dear husband.

"Don, I don't know what this says about me as a wife or a person, but I was kind of getting a kick out of watching the EMG today," I told him. "I think I might be enjoying it a little too much."

That was the easier of the tests they ran. We had lots more that made laughing a little harder to do. When they got ready to do his spinal tap, I sat and held his hands. Don, who didn't get worked up by much, turned pale and broke out into a sweat as we waited for a doctor to come in and get things going. I think it was mostly nerves, but there we were wrestling with so many emotions over the few days we were in Houston as Don went through one test after another. And remember, this was just to rule things out since ALS cannot be tested for. That meant rather than taking one test for the disease, he had to test for every disease to make sure that it wasn't something else. He was starting to feel like a real guinea pig when it was all said and done. They even gave him a psychiatric test. He had to look at cards and tell the doctor what he saw in these weird ink blots. Don had about had it with tests by then, but I thought it was kind of enjoyable—like looking at clouds and trying to figure out what they're shaped like. So I sat there with him and tried to figure out what I thought the blobs were. We were never seeing the same things! I wasn't surprised. If our battles over what color of flowers to plant in the yard had taught me anything, it was that Don and I saw things just a little bit differently. But as they say, opposites attract! Anyway, about a third of the way through, Don got a little put out.

"Look, I'm finished with this test. I don't need to take something like this. I'm not crazy. I'm having a hard time walking!"

The doctor agreed to forgo the rest of that test. Personally I was a little disappointed. First, it was the only test that didn't involve needles or prodding, and second, I was kind of enjoying it.

As we went through one test after the next, I was just praying every time they did a new one that someone would come in and say, "Well, look at that. It was a pinched nerve all along. Sorry about all the fuss. I guess we made a mistake." I was hoping for the world's worst mix-up. But that isn't what happened. There'd been no mix-up or oversight. The hunch the very first doctor had was right. Don was in the beginning stages of ALS. In fact, he'd been living with it for a year already. It had started when the limping started.

Of all the bad news that we got in Houston, there was a strange kind of silver lining to it all. In all the tests they did on Don, they found that his lungs were in great shape, functioning at 100 percent. The doctors explained to us that this was a good thing; it meant that he was at very least starting out from the best starting point he could. There was another blessing in disguise that came of all this. Over the last month or so, I had noticed Don twitching an awful lot. It was so bad that I could feel his muscles twitching at night when we lay in bed. It was like there was a small dance party or popcorn popping going on just under Don's skin. When I noticed how bad it had gotten, it worried me. When the doctors confirmed that Don had ALS, my worry went into high gear. I was sure that the twitching must have been a bad sign. But as it turned out, the twitching was actually a good thing.

"So far all the research on ALS has shown that men with good lungs and the twitching are more likely to live longer with this debilitating disease," the doctor told us. "So while I know this is hardly reason to celebrate, you really are coming into this from the best place possible."

"Aren't you glad I never took up smoking, Lynda Sue?" Don said with a little grin.

All there was to do after the diagnosis was one last round of giving blood; the last time, however, it was for research rather than diagnosis. Because there is still no cure for the disease, specialists everywhere take samples from patients to try to get to the bottom of what causes ALS and how to cure it. And with that, our time in Houston was nearly complete. Although it was hardly what one would call a good trip, Don and I could not have been better taken care of. From the time we checked in to the time we left, the hospital was outstanding in every possible way, and Don's doctor was the best in the field.

Before we left, Rod and Pam prayed with us one last time, and we headed back home. It was a strange trip. I spent the entire time working through a gamut of emotions. Don just kept telling me it would all be okay. I couldn't figure out how—if my best friend, my husband of nearly thirty years, my soul mate had ALS—anything would ever be okay, but Don insisted. And something about his strength gave me strength. Although he did certainly go through his own bouts of sorrow, he always pulled himself back together and assured me that everything would be okay.

"This isn't ideal," he said, "but God won't give us anything we can't handle. We'll be okay."

We pulled into our driveway after dark that evening. It felt good to be home, but it also felt a little strange. It was like we were walking into the same house we left the week before as two different people. You really do kind of become a different person after a diagnosis like Don's. I mean, life is never the same after something like that. Everything feels a little different—every holiday, every vacation, every child born. With every celebration, there is a twinge of sadness that follows the joy because you know in the back of your mind that you may not have many more birthdays or Christmases or family vacations left. But you know, that also makes every single moment that much more precious. It makes it so that you soak up every second and you don't let any memory slip by you. Don, ever the one to be strong and faithful, even in the darkest of times, had this to say, or write, about the diagnosis a few months after it came:

> I have never been a person that adjusts to changes very easily. My family knows that I am very predictable, practical, dependable and I like to know what is being planned. As I drive to work each morning, I use this time to pray; for forgiveness, give praise to our heavenly Father, for my family, friends, and the needs of others.
>
> This day was different,. I realized how routine my prayer time had become, I knew that there were changes that needed to be made. The last four months our lives have been changed not the way we had planned but in a new direction. Being diagnosed with ALS is hard to deal with, and I know that this is the easy time for me with this disease. Lynda and I have talked about what a peace we have, not that we look forward to the difficult days but God has given us a new focus. In Matthew 7, verse 24 Jesus talks about building a house on a strong foundation or building a house on sand and how the storms of life affect each one. It is amazing at different times in our lives how God's word will speak to our hearts.
>
> I have taken for granted the ability to stand, walk, talk, eat, kneel, shake a friend's hand or give a hug. Today I have made a commitment to not take for granted what the Lord has given to me and

what he has done for me, by kneeling in prayer as a privilege to speak to our heavenly Father.

This peace and strength that Lynda and I have comes from our relationship with our Lord and Savior, your prayers and kindness that you show our family.

Thank you for your support and prayers,

—Don Strahorn

In a way, I wished that I could have lived my whole life the way we lived after Don was diagnosed, grateful for every small thing that happened. I had come to just expect Don to always be there. Of course, I loved him and appreciated him, but I just took for granted that we'd grow old together—that we'd have decades of watching grandkids and even great-grandkids growing up. When we found out that we had limited time together, I quit taking the little things for granted, and I began to cling to every tiny memory. It's like I felt things more intensely when that happened.

"Home again, home again," I said as we walked in the door.

"I think we got a problem, babe," Don said as he walked in the house.

"I'd say so," I murmured, thinking he was referring to the ALS.

"Look up," he said.

I guess God thought we needed something to take our minds off Don's disease because we arrived home that night to a house full of leaks. It was spring in Oklahoma, which meant thunderstorms and high winds. While we were gone, a storm had come through and did a real number on our roof. As we walked through the house, we found one leak after the next. Don's office had so much water in it I thought I might need a lifejacket to go in and start the cleanup. When it was all said and done, I filled the Shop-Vac up over a dozen times. There were also leaks in the dining room.

"Looks like we need a new roof, Lynda Sue," Don said as he helped me lug the Shop-Vac to the sink.

The night after we got back, the storm chasers were out and about. For anyone who hasn't grown up in Tornado Alley, this is a sign that a tornado is on the way. All the news stations send out their storm chasers to track tornadoes across the state. If you've ever seen the movie *Twister*, that's a storm chaser. When I saw on the news that they were anticipating tornadoes, my daughter Jaclyn called to say that they were going to come and bunker down at our house. That had been the protocol for some time when the weather got ugly.

"I don't know if you and Clint want to come here, sweetie," I told her.

"Why not?"

"Because with the way things are going for us lately, our house is probably right on the path of the storm!"

As luck would have it, we were not hit by a tornado that night, but we did have quite a journey in front of us, and it had so many ups and downs that it was dizzying at times. God prepared our hearts for all of it, however. We are lucky to have a God that loves and cares about us the way He does. There is nothing that could ever compare to that love. And we were lucky to have friends constantly there reminding us of that love. That's another positive that came from all this; we saw how loved Don and our family was. We always knew we had amazing people in our lives, but the following are stories that demonstrate that in the weeks following our arrival home from Houston.

Fall 2008

3

My Name Is Lynda,
I'm Thankful for…So Much

While we were in Houston with the best ALS doctor in the country, we found out that there was actually a doctor in Oklahoma City who had studied under our Houston specialist, so when we got back we made an appointment to meet this doctor to find out what our next step was going to be. We fit perfectly with the doctor and his staff, which was a good thing because for the next seven years we would be seeing them every three months.

Our first meeting started out a little rough, but not because of the staff or the doctor. After we checked in, the first thing they did was put us in a room with an EMG machine. Don and I looked at the machine, and I think we both about hit the floor. When the doctor walked in, Don was waiting and ready with his first comment.

"I've had three of those tests done already, and I don't plan to have another!" he told the doctor.

The doctor smiled in response and explained that Don did not have a date with the EMG machine that day. We were just doing the appointment in that room. I think we both let out a sigh of relief.

The appointments became a bit like clockwork after the first one. Every time we would go in, we would meet with the doctor, a nurse, a respiratory therapist, someone from MDA, and an occupational therapist. We came prepared with questions, and the staff came ready to answer them all. Before all the appointments, there was always about a thirty-minute wait. Don and I sat side by side in the waiting room doing our best not to stare at other patients, but it was hard not to. We knew we were looking at our future, and it was not the kind of future that you've got to wear shades for, if you know what I mean. This was like looking into a hole of gloom and doom. Needless to say, we didn't see much hope in that waiting room. What we did get out of the visits, however, was the name of a support group for ALS that met monthly. Of course we thought we needed to take advantage of what they had to offer. We weren't sure what it was that they had to offer, but we went to the next one they had to find out.

When we pulled into the parking lot to go to the support group meeting, I could feel my stomach turning. It seemed more nerve-racking thinking about going into that building than it did walking into the hospital in Houston to get the initial tests. Don put the car in park, and we just sat there staring at the front door like it was the mouth of some giant monster that wanted to swallow us whole. A few minutes went by, and Don looked from the front door to me. I could tell he felt the same way I was feeling. We didn't say a word. We just sat quietly and watched. It's like we were waiting for someone to tell us what to do next. God knows in some ways we were.

As we sat dumbfounded by this new situation we found ourselves in, other cars started pulling into the empty parking spaces around us. People started to get out of their SUVS, sedans, and minivans. I noticed that almost all the vehicles had handicap license plates. I also noticed that most of the people going in were using scooters or wheelchairs. At that moment, I got sucker punched from reality. It would be us with the handicap decal and the wheelchair before long. I could almost feel the wind come out of me.

"I don't want to go in," Don blurted, as he looked over at me, looking at all these people rolling into the meeting.

"Well, we have to, so let's get out of this car and *walk* in there while we still can!" I told him, emphasis on the world *walk*.

We looked and felt like two kids on their first day at a new school. It was like the waiting room, but on steroids. Again, I did my best not to stare at the couples that were there that night, but all I could think was *Here's our future, and I'm scared*. I tried to get past my fear so I could concentrate on the meeting and what was being said. The following are the things I learned that night:

1. I am now a *caregiver*—not just a wife, but a caregiver.
2. They have devices to speak for you when you lose your voice.
3. You can use a child's Magna Doodle to write on when your speech is slurred and you need to communicate.
4. We were not alone on this journey.

As much information as we got that night, the one thing that blew me away the most was when the man next to me said that he had just gotten his chair and it cost thirty-five thousand dollars! My jaw about hit the floor. I turned to Don and whispered, "Did you hear that! Did you hear that!?" I was sure I must've misheard him, so I had to clarify. I turned to the man and asked, "How much did you say your chair cost?" I didn't have to look at Don to feel him shaking his head at me. After being married almost thirty years, he had to have seen that coming from a mile away. I am not one to keep my questions to myself.

"Well, this one has all the bells and whistles, and so these kind run from thirty-two thousand to forty thousand dollars."

I searched that thing over with my eyes at least four times, and I didn't see one bell or whistle on that thing! For that much, I thought it ought to have gold spokes, an espresso machine, and a masseuse attached to the back of it, but it looked like a run-of-the-mill electric wheelchair to me. I knew right then that we were in trouble. We had never even owned a car that cost that much!

We learned a lot at support group and developed many friendships, some of which wouldn't last long because our new friend would pass away so quickly. We learned about noninvasive respirators versus life support, how to lift someone who had fallen, feeding tubes, and on and on. It could get pretty bleak talking about what to expect when your muscles are atrophying by the day, so as we finished every meeting, we would go around the room and each of us would have to tell something we were thankful for. I noticed that most of the people there with ALS would always say they were thankful for their spouses or loved ones who were caring for them. They were totally dependent on these people to take care of all their needs. I'm sure this is why every time I would go somewhere, Don would say, "Please be careful. Drive safely. I don't think I can make this journey without you." Not that he wasn't always caring and worried about my safety, but I became his sole source of security.

Our daughters went to a few meetings with us and met several of the families going through the same thing we were. They sat and listened as everyone in the group said what they were thankful for. Sometimes they smiled, and sometimes they cried. Our boys, on the other hand, were a little harder to get to the meetings. We finally talked them into going to one in May, during ALS awareness month.

This was about a year into the diagnosis, so they were still sorting out their feelings about all of it. Instead of being at a medical building or a community center, this meeting was held at a nice restaurant, which I figured would make it a bit easier for the boys. The doctor, nurse, and facilitator who lead the group were all there and had asked everyone to bring their families to this meeting. Even with it being at a restaurant, the boys were a little apprehensive about coming, but they eventually caved.

As we were going around making introductions, I was introducing Ryan to someone very special to us. I said, "Ryan, I would like you to meet Susan."

"Hi, Susan. It's nice to meet you," he said as he held out his hand to shake hers. What he didn't know was Susan, who had been diagnosed just one week before Don, had already lost the ability to speak and could not move her arms anymore. Since she couldn't raise her arms, she swung one arm at him and said, "Nice to meet you!" Her words were slurred and a little hard to understand, like someone who had suffered a severe stroke.

Susan handled it beautifully. She smiled and hugged him by laying her head on his chest. Ryan was not as graceful in the situation. He immediately turned around, sat down in his chair, and didn't move again for the rest of the evening. I guess it hadn't occurred to me what it would be like for him. Don and I had been slowly adjusting to everything, but Ryan was just kind of thrown into the deep end. Sometimes, though, that is the only way we learn to swim.

As the evening went on, we went around the table and said what we were thankful for. Don and I were both thankful to have all four of our children there that night. Jaclyn handled it like a pro and said what she was thankful for. Jennifer cried as she talked about how strong her dad was. Ryan followed our lead and said he was thankful to spend time with us and his siblings, and then there was Jonathan.

"I'm just thankful my dad's ALS started in his foot because from what I understand, that means his will move slower than someone whose starts in the mouth or upper body," he said as we all sat, eyes wide and unblinking, listening to him.

When he was done with his little speech, we all just dropped our heads. What Jonathan didn't know was that all the ALS patients' disease sitting around the table listening to him there that night had started in their upper body or their speech, which is called *bulbar ALS*. The one thing that I learned, though, is that it doesn't matter where it starts. ALS doesn't care where or when it hits next; no two cases are alike.

When we left there that night, Jonathan looked at Ryan and said, "I can't believe you tried to shake that woman's hand!"

Ryan came back at him and said, "Well, you pretty much told everyone in there that they're goners!" Needless to say, the boys never came back to another support group meeting, and I think we were all thankful for that!

Don and me with the kids and grandkids

Jennifer, Don and Jaclyn

4

Friends Are Family that You Choose

The first year of ALS was a whirlwind of emotions for all our family and friends. That support group we were so hesitant about walking into that first day was a real lifesaver for us in so many ways, although it was also heartbreaking and terrifying at times since we were losing friends to ALS every time we turned around. As much of a reality check as it was though, I strongly recommend support groups to anyone who is facing a terminal illness.

Another bittersweet aspect of the diagnosis was the way our friends came through for us. I mean to tell you, I had never felt so loved in my life. I always knew we had amazing friends, but once Don was diagnosed, people came out of the woodwork to support us in unbelievable ways. Perhaps the most incredible thing our friends did was put together a 5K fund-raiser for us that first year. They called it "4Don@ Dusk," and they held the first fun run on the first Saturday in May, which is ALS awareness month. After they decided to do the fund-raiser, they started having meetings to figure out the details. The first meeting was held at the Cordray's home, just to brainstorm ways that we might raise money for all the costs of ALS. Jennifer and Jaclyn planned on going, but Jen ended up calling me before the meeting saying that she wanted to come up with an excuse not to go. I know the girls were having trouble with these things because they were reminders that Don was sick and all they wanted was for things to stay the same. I felt pretty much the same way. But as Jen and I talked, we both realized that there was no reason not to go, except for the most obvious fact that it meant facing this thing head on.

"I just can't do it, Mom," she told me. "I just want Dad to be the same dad that walked me down the aisle. If I go, it reminds me he's not."

Jen and Jaclyn both ended up staying home from that first meeting, but Don and I faced our fears and went. We showed up to the meeting an hour after it started to give whoever was there a little time to talk about things before we arrived. That was Don; he wanted to make sure that he didn't make anyone feel uncomfortable. I think we were both kind of dreading it the way we had dreaded the first support group meeting. It just made the diagnosis that much more real. But when we pulled up to the house, we were speechless when we saw the amount of cars that lined the street. All my anxiety and hesitation melted away as I entered a house full of familiar and loving faces. There were people from church, some friends that we'd been close to since high school, friends of the kids, and ministers of our church. Really, it was our family—the family that we chose rather than the family we were born with.

We sat and listened to everyone coming up with different ideas to help raise money for Don. Their first goal was to get our bathrooms handicap accessible. As I took it all in—all these people who had taken time out of their day to be there and get this thing going—I was totally taken aback; Don was too. I knew we had great people in our life, but still, I was overwhelmed by how much everyone loved and cared for both of us and by how everyone wanted to help in any way possible. I cried until 1:00 a.m. that night, but that night, I cried tears of joy because I was so very grateful for all the people God had put in our lives.

They put the whole thing together using Facebook and word of mouth. Don and I had grown up in the Midwest City and Del City areas, and we had been members of our church for thirty-two years at that time, so the gathering ended up being much larger than anyone had expected, although it would continue to grow over the years. That very first one I will never forget though. It was cloudy that day and rain was coming down in all the surrounding cities around us, but somehow the rain did not fall on us that day. We were a little dry spot in all the rain. At the finish line hung a huge banner that said "4Don@Dusk Annual

5K Walk/Run." Team Strahorn, as they called themselves, were all clad in blue shirts that they had made. All the participants that day wore white, and all the family was in red. A fire engine that was there signaled the beginning of the race, and everyone in white took off, some faster than others. Don and I headed the pack with our granddaughter Carlie in a golf cart. We all wore our bright red shirts and huge smiles that day. There was upbeat music playing over loud speakers to keep everyone's spirits high, and spirits were certainly that! You couldn't help but feel the love when you walked into something like that. I couldn't have been sad if I tried that day. All of Team Strahorn had worked endlessly to make things perfect, and they were absolutely successful. The whole thing could not have gone any better. I think we were all overwhelmed by all the love and support we received that day.

At the end of the first annual 4Don@Dusk fun run (which our friends went on to do every year on the first Saturday of May), our amazing friends had raised twenty-two thousand dollars! We had surpassed our goal by a landslide, which meant we could get the bathrooms renovated and made handicap accessible. I tell you what, I couldn't have been more overwhelmed with joy and gratitude if Ed McMahan showed up at my door with one of those giant checks for millions. It wasn't just about the money they had raised, which would be used to pay for ramps, leg braces, wheelchairs, and piling medical bills that came with an ALS diagnosis. I was overjoyed because that money demonstrated to Don and me that we were not alone in this fight. We had an entire community behind us, rooting us on, ready and willing to do whatever we needed the minute we said the word. I cannot stress enough how critical having that community has been.

Our friends went on to throw different fund-raisers and just plain pitch in whenever they could the entire time. After 4Don@Dusk, the same group put on a Family Fun Day at the Cordray's home. There was food, games, live music, and fireworks—all to raise money for Don. We all had a great day, but I had no doubt that we would. Don and I got there at three o'clock and found all our friends fast at work and getting ready for everyone to arrive. Some were in the kitchen working on the food, and others were setting up tables, moonwalks, and a stage for the bands. Others were making cotton candy, popcorn, and snow cones. We all sat down to watch the Blue Angels fly. When Jonathan got there, he had a big laugh at how we all looked so old sitting under a tree looking up at the sky and pointing every time a plane would fly over, like we'd never seen one before.

So many friends and family showed up that day. We had live music and karaoke with some of the kids. We realized that day that Carlie is a little like her aunts and likes to sing, but we decided it was time to teach her some more songs because all she sang was "Twinkle, Twinkle Little Star" about eight times in a row. Jonathan and his band also played, but after only one song, a storm came rolling in. I have never seen so many people move so fast, but we were still having fun. When Don and I left the Cordray's that night, Don looked over at me and said, "This was so much fun today that I forgot that they were doing this for me and why they were doing it."

I needed that network of friends from our church and community like never before. See, if you ask anyone to describe me, there's a good bet you'll hear words like "upbeat," "positive," "happy," and maybe even "loud." But after Don was diagnosed, I started to kind of feel that part of me being overpowered by sadness and grief. I wasn't angry, really; I was just more confused than I'd ever been. Some days it felt like I couldn't tell up from down anymore. And it didn't help that the most doctors could tell us was eventually a number of awful things may or may not happen. Because ALS affects everyone differently, we had no idea what to expect. Don, being the true Boy Scout that he was, did his homework as much as he possibly could so we would be prepared. Problem was, there was no telling what lay ahead of us. Some people died within a year of diagnosis, while others would live for five or six. I'll never forget the strangest and most awful question I ever had to hear Don ask.

"I need to know, Doc," he said. "How do people die of ALS? I mean, what is going to end up killing me?"

I thought, *My gosh, Don! What a morbid question to ask!* I was waiting for the doctor's facial expression to show the shock I felt, but it never did. At the end of the day, the fact was we needed to be asking those tough questions. Because the truth of the matter was, it was going to happen whether or not we asked. We couldn't hide from ALS or ignore it. It was the elephant in the room everywhere we went. Don knew that the best way to handle it all was to be ready for it. He didn't want to be surprised by anything if he could avoid it. So he just came out and asked, "How am I gonna kick the bucket?"

"You will likely die one of three ways: choke to death, pneumonia, or carbon monoxide will build up and you will just slip away.

"Well, I'll take the third one," Don said, like he had a choice in the matter. I was thinking the same exact thing as he said it though.

"Well, you certainly can't choke to death!" I told him.

We laughed whenever we could, but there were times that I couldn't muster a smile. My bubbly mood would fade away as I thought about the moment that what Don was asking would come to pass. I would realize time and again that this disease was going to take him—that I would be a widow way before I was old enough to be one—and I could feel all my happiness just vanish into thin air. I know my kids could tell the difference in my mood. Jaclyn even wrote a short entry on Don's CarePage about it. I knew that our future was in God's hands, and I prayed and prayed for peace, which God did continue to grant me. But there were still times it was really hard to hold back the tears. In the beginning especially, I just wished Don would start hopping around on both feet and shout, "April Fools!" Granted, I may have inflicted injury on him for that kind of joke, but I would have given anything to wake up from that nightmare. It wasn't a joke though. It was the most serious thing we'd ever faced. And I couldn't have done it without so much support.

So the fact was, the whole thing felt like a bad dream. I told my daughters daily that was exactly what it felt like—a bad dream that I couldn't wake up from. But we weren't going to let what time Don had left to be filled with gloom and grief. While he was still with us, we decided we were going to do all we could to celebrate his life. We were on a mission to rack up as many memories as we could, so a couple of months after his diagnosis, we went to Las Vegas with the kids, went on a cruise with our friends the Cordrays, and went to Florida for a vacation with some high school friends. And there were great friends who offered us their home in Colorado, which we took our whole family to, all seventeen of us, and visited two years in a row. We were going to do all we could while Don could still travel, and we included everyone we could to help make every trip that much more special.

Don and I made a lot of memories that first year, but we also hit some pretty dark places, which is inevitable. Neither of us slept at all that first year after he was diagnosed. I just powered through it, but Don's insomnia got so bad the doctor prescribed him Ambien to help him get to sleep. We found out during that time that you don't always fall asleep and remember things after waking when taking Ambien. When Don popped that Ambien in his mouth that night, I figured it would relax him and he would just doze off. I had no idea a person could share very intimate moments, if you catch my drift, while on the sleep medication. When we woke up the next day, Don had no idea what had happened the night before. I thought he was being romantic, but he was in an Ambien delirium the entire time!

The following morning, I woke up to Don gently rubbing my back and asking me if I felt like making love. My eyes popped open, and I turned over and said, "WHAT? Really? Are you kidding?!"

I could see he was baffled by my reaction, making both of us equally confused. We were a scene right out of *I Love Lucy*. You know the scenarios, where Ricky and Lucy think they're talking about the same thing but they aren't and chaos ensues? That was us that morning. I sat up and said, "What about last night?!"

"What?" he said. He had no idea what I was talking about. He didn't remember a thing. That will be a memory only I will ever have. Well, sort of. What I thought was a very beautiful and *private* moment turned out to be anything but private. Don thought it was just hysterical once he realized what had gone on. He shared it with all our friends, which was so unlike him. And where most women could say, "Not tonight, honey. I have a headache," I could just tell Don that we had made mad, passionate love the night before right after he took his pill and he just didn't remember. We got a good chuckle out of that.

Along with the sleeplessness, there were also the moments of quiet that were so hard to deal with. When we'd go to dinner at one of the kid's houses or out with friends, we would do okay, other than being pretty worn down. But it seemed like the minute it was just the two of us alone, all we could talk about was ALS and what the future held. That was when it was hardest on us.

"I'm afraid that when it gets to the point that I have to be in a wheelchair or I can't talk that I'm going to scare my own grandkids," Don told me one night as we lay in bed. We had two grandkids at that time, Carlie and Harison. Having grandkids was one of Don's greatest pleasures in the world. It tore my heart out to see the worry in his eyes that one day he would frighten them instead of comfort them.

"They won't be scared of you!" I insisted. "You're their Papa! You'll just have new accessories when you have a wheelchair."

Jaclyn wrote the following about her reaction to ALS the first year that I think sums up Don's sentiment well:

What I have heard dad say that he wanted to do most is see his kids grow up, and selfishly I want him to be around to someday see my kids grow up too. Today is the first day, since we found out the diagnosis, that I realized what this really means, and it has been hard on me. There is no better dad than my daddy, and it is hard for me to understand the reasoning behind all of this, but like we sang in the Easter musical this morning "I am not skilled to understand, what God has willed, what God has planned." And all I could think while singing this morning was to praise God for dying on the cross so that one day, when I die I will be reunited with my daddy.

And then there was Don's take on the whole thing. The following is Don's first post on his CarePage from April 2007, just a month after he was diagnosed, which I end this chapter with because it sums up beautifully the ups and downs we experienced as well as what got us through it all:

I was wondering how to start this update and remembered when Rod Harnden asked me to teach his Sunday School class. This was something that I had to step out of my comfort zone & claim Philippians 4:13, (I can do all things through Him who strengthens me). Now you have to understand that I never spoke in class and Lynda always did. I stepped in front of the class & said, "Hello, my name is Don Strahorn, and I am the person that has been sitting by Lynda for the past year, and that sums up how our relationship works."

I want to thank you for your support, prayers, friendships and the love you have shown our family. I told Jaclyn when it was a possibility that I had ALS that we were not going to ask why, because I know that God did not cause this to happen. I do know that God can work miracles and that He can work things for good to those who love the Lord. Our family is and has been blessed, and is still being blessed even during these difficult times. I'm not saying that is not difficult because it is, but I know that we are not the only family that goes through difficult situations, and every time I feel sorry for myself I am reminded in some way with that realization. Honestly I do not know how I would cope with this if I did not have my family, friends and utmost my relationship and faith in my Lord, Jesus. One last verse that I claim every day is Proverbs 3:5-6, "Trust in the Lord with all your heart, do not lean on your own understanding but in all ways acknowledge him, and he will make your paths straight."

Again thank you for all of your support because we do feel & appreciate it.

With all of our love & thanks.

—Don Strahorn

Needless to say, Don and I were always reassured at how our family is loved and blessed when we needed that reassurance most. The Lord blessed us with so many Christian friends, a wonderful family, and even good doctors. In that difficult time, it was so nice to know that we had such a good support system and prayers coming from all directions.

Don and me on a trip with friends

4Don@Dusk

Me, Don, Marcheta and Mark

5

What to Expect When You're Expecting...ALS

So many things changed for our family in the first year of Don's diagnosis. It's funny how something like that really brings into focus what is really important, what needs to get done, and most importantly, making sure we spend all the time we had the best way possible. For Don and me, our walk with the Lord became first and foremost in our lives. Our faith had always been central to our family and lives, but we were calling on God like we never had. We were also always thinking about how this might bring others closer to the Lord.

After God, spending time with our family was the next priority, not that we hadn't always spent a lot of time with our children and parents. Most of us lived in the same town, if not the same neighborhood! We never had any problems thinking up a reason to have a get-together. It might be a birthday, a holiday, a weekend, or just any old night of the week we felt like it. In fact, someone once told me we were an odd kind of family.

"Odd?" I asked. Sure, *I* knew that we were odd, but I didn't know what this person meant because they'd never seen a Strahorn get-together firsthand to know how odd we were.

"Well, you know, it's just most people want to be with their friends, but you all just want to be with your family. It's a good thing, don't get me wrong! Most families don't enjoy each other's company enough to spend that much time together."

It was true; we did enjoy getting together for any reason we could think of. But after the diagnosis, the time became so much more precious. Don had always been a wonderful and dedicated son to his parents. He checked in on them all the time and did all he could to spend time with them whenever possible. He wasn't the kind that just checked in for holidays and birthdays, that is for sure. But after we got that terrible, life-altering news, he would go by to visit his parents almost every day to reassure them, soak up his time with them, and love them.

In October 2012, only fourteen months before Don passed away, my father-in-law, Jack, had a heart attack and died. Our family pulled together and surrounded my mother-in-law with love. The months after that, Don checked on his mom daily and would call her every night to see if she needed anything and just to see how her day was. "Do you need anything, Mom? Is there anything you need help with?" I would hear him saying on the phone. I would just listen and smile at him as I thought, *Geez Louise, Don, how in the world are you going to help her?* I knew if she said she needed something though, he would have found a way; he always did.

After Jack passed away, we saw DewAnn (that is, my mother-in-law) almost daily. As Don was trying to take care of her, she was sneaking around and taking care of him instead. She would bring us lunch or dinner, pick up something from the store that she thought we needed, or just stop by for a few minutes to see her youngest son. I eventually had to tell her, "DewAnn, you know our door is always open to you! You don't have to bring something to come by!"

If I have any advice to someone who is going through this, it is to make sure that your door is open to the people who love you. Don't shut them out and try to do this alone. I would put myself in DewAnn's place and think about if this were my son or daughter, where would I want to be? Right by their sides, that's where! That is all DewAnn wanted too, and I wasn't going to take that from her. She deserved her time with her son. I owed her that; she was a big reason he was the man he was. Sometimes when she would come over toward the end, I would try to keep myself busy doing things around the house to give them some special quality time. On several occasions, I would come in to find her and Don both asleep, just napping in the same room, as peaceful as can be. Now that would always put a smile on my face. She was right where she needed to be.

My in-laws were definitely two big blessings the Lord had given me, and I was going to let my mother-in-law live there if she wanted to at that point. She and Jack were wonderful examples as both parents and grandparents for Don and me. I had the amazing family I did because they brought Don up in a way that made him an amazing dad and an unbelievable husband. I can't say how grateful I was for them, for their love, encouragement, and guidance throughout our lives, and for their support when we needed it most. To tell the truth though, when Don was diagnosed, I think we worried about them as much as we did Don's disease. We knew that it was almost unbearable for them. Don was the baby of the family. Neither his mom nor his dad could stand to think of him sick and, God forbid, of a world without him in it. Don had a really hard time telling them at first, in fact. That's something you don't really think about until you have to do it—how hard it is to tell your mom and dad that their son or daughter has a terminal illness. Truly, telling the family was about as terrible as hearing the news to begin with.

Then there were our children—where do I start? Ryan, our firstborn, would call Don not just daily but several times a day just to talk and to see if he needed anything done. Jennifer, who has always been and continues to be the one who takes care of business and gets things done, constantly reassured me that we were going to be okay. "I'm always here for you, Mom," she'd tell me again and again. It was like we were trading roles in a way. I had spent so much time nurturing her, taking care of her, kissing her bumps and bruises, and telling her that she'd be okay. Suddenly, she was the one soothing me. Then there was Jaclyn, who is my sensitive one—always has been. She is quiet but hears everything and just absorbs it. She was a little more fragile at first, just because her heart is so gentle. But she was the one who could always express how we were feeling with words on the CarePages. Finally, we have Jonathan, my comedian, who always tried to lighten up the situation. But I knew, and so did Don, that underneath all the wisecracks and one-liners, he was hurting. I was just so glad that all of them had chosen amazing, God-sent spouses that not only fit into our circus of a family but could also support my kids through the hardest time of their lives.

We also had two little blessings, our grandchildren, Carlie and Harison. They were our proof that the Lord does indeed have a sense of humor. Carlie acts just like her Grammy (that's me); bless her heart, she knows no stranger and never shuts her mouth. I once asked my little Carlie if she knew what was wrong with Papa. As sure as she could be, she told me, "Yes, he has ASS."

"Exactly!" I told her, clapping my hands, tickled at the kind of levity a five-year-old can bring to any situation without even trying.

Harison, on the other hand, acted just like his Papa (Don). While Carlie was running around singing or picking on her Papa and Grammy, Harison was quiet, kind, and loving. They brought so much joy to our lives. And Don brought so much joy into their lives. Because of that, when the girls found out Don had ALS, they both decided they wanted to have kids as soon as they could so Don would be able to see them and so their kids would get to know their Papa. Before the diagnosis, we had two grandchildren, Carlie and Harison. After the diagnosis, our girls got busy, and we had five more grandkids within three years! That put us at three granddaughters and four grandsons. But with ALS, everything became a little bittersweet. See, where the grandkids and announcements of new grandbabies on the way had always been a point of celebration, after the diagnosis, the cold, hard reality that Don wouldn't be around to see these grandbabies have their own babies made for some pretty tough times.

In November 2007, we found out that Jaclyn and Clint were expecting twins. Our family was so excited about having twin grandsons. At around the same time the twins came the following summer, Jennifer and Jeremy announced they were expecting a baby. With every announcement, my heart grew and ached at the same time. Yet another thing you don't consider until you have been handed a life sentence.

I realized that we weren't alone in what we were going through with the ups and downs that came with these kinds of blessings. One day in a support group meeting, I listened to our dear friend Susan (you remember her from the Ryan incident), she talked about how excited she was that she had just found out that she was going to be a grandmother.

"I just hope and pray that the Lord will let me have the ability to speak and hold my grandbaby," she told the group.

My heart went out to her. As a woman and a grandmother, I understood how much it meant to be able to tell them how much you love them and to hug, hold, and cuddle those precious little ones.

The further Don progressed, the more painful the realizations became for both of us—especially him. I remember the day we found out Jonathan and Brandy were going to have a baby. We were all at my brother's house in July for a family swim party. Jonathan and Brandy called everyone together so they could make their big announcement.

"Well, there's going to be another little one in the family," they told us. "We are having a baby in March!"

It was such a surprise to all of us, and everyone was so excited to hear that. At first, I was elated. I immediately thought about how we'd have eight grandkids in no time. Our house was crazy as it was! And it was about to get one grandkid crazier! With so many grandkids there came lots of noise, craziness, and joy at our house because the kids and grandkids were at our house all the time. They were our pride and joy. But being our pride and joy did not guarantee perfection or good behavior all the time. Sometimes the house was loud and messy, but it was also fun! There were also fights in the pews at church that we'd have to break up as one of the boys threatened his older brother trying to put a booger on him. And one of my favorites, when our little Emily, dressed as pretty as could be in her little Cinderella dress, popped up at the backdoor. We'd all been sitting around the table, having a great, adult conversation. The weather was nice so the kids were all outside, giving us the rare opportunity to chat without constant interruptions of "Mom!" or "Grammy!" or "Papa!"

When we looked over to see what she needed, we noticed there was something in her mouth. On further inspection, we all realized that she was clenching her princess panties between her teeth. Now that is not what I expected her to be chewing on when she walked up!

"I am so glad it's not my kid this time!" Ryan said as he burst out into laughter.

Jennifer jumped up from the table ran to the door. "Emily, why are your panties in your mouth?" she asked as she shook her head in disbelief.

"Because I poo pooed," Emily told her very matter-of-factly, like that was as good an explanation as any for carrying around your drawers in your mouth.

"Where?" Jennifer exclaimed.

Emily didn't have to answer. All the other kids pointed and said, "Over there!"

"Emily, sweetheart," I said after I caught my breath from the laughter. "All that Cinderella left behind was a shoe!"

I couldn't wait to add another to the mix. Then I wondered what it would be. As I imagined a new little boy and then a new little girl, that's when it hit me. I started counting months in my head; March was eight months away. At that point, Don had been getting weaker and weaker since March that year. I didn't know if he would make it another eight months.

When Don and I got in the van that day, I looked over at him and said, "Well, how about that? Another grandbaby."

Don had tears in his eyes when he said, "Lynda, I don't think I'm going to be around to see that baby."

I didn't want to say the words out loud, but I had already thought the same thing. The rest of the drive home, neither of us uttered a word. We were left with that looming thought. And suddenly, it wasn't just that Don wouldn't meet our newest addition. It was that Don wouldn't be here at all anymore. That he'd never see another birthday or Christmas. That he'd never go to another pool party or see another firework show. In all the books written about what to expect when you're expecting a new baby, they don't ever tell you how to handle the heart-wrenching emotions of what to expect when you're expecting a baby and your loved one has ALS. They also don't tell you that some of the tears you cry when that happens won't be tears of joy, or that a baby announcement in some ways becomes a reminder that you don't know how long you have with a person that makes your world go round.

A month or so after we found out about the baby, I told Brandy what Don had said. It was not an easy conversation to have, but I had to tell her. It had been weighing on my heart since the day he said it. In October, less than three months before Don would take his very last breath, Brandy came over to the house after the big appointment. You know the one, where they make sure everything is going well and tell you if you need to start buying pink booties or blue ones. Well, she and Jonathan had decided that they would be buying yellow booties until the baby made his or her big debut. They weren't going to find out the sex; instead, they wanted to be surprised. But that wouldn't be the only surprise Brandy had up her sleeve.

That day at the doctor's office, Brandy had the ultrasound technician slip an ultrasound that revealed the sex of the baby inside an envelope. She left the office that day and came right over to our house, where she presented Don with a sealed envelope. He looked at it and looked at her.

"You are going to be the only one who knows the sex of the baby," she told him with a teary-eyed smile.

What a gift she gave him that day! He needed help opening the envelope because of his hands. Once I helped him with the envelope, he took the paper out and read it, with a huge smile planted on his face. He decided he would call that baby Pat after that, from *Saturday Night Live* fame. And Don kept that secret all those months, even though everyone kept trying to get it out of him. He said nothing to anyone until the night before he died. Brandy came in and told Don, "You can tell Lynda. I know you want someone to talk about the baby with."

"A boy would be nice," he told me with a knowing grin. "But a girl is just so much prettier."

Those were beautiful and impossible times. Don loved his grandkids so much, even when they were destroying the house. The grandkids would always jump on the couch, so Don demanded he go to his kids' house and do the same. I reminded him in a wheelchair there wasn't much jumping on a couch he'd be doing.

"Well, take me over there. You take all the cushions off the couch and put them on the floor, and I'll roll around on the cushions," he told me with his famous little grin. "That's how I'll jump on their couch!" He was also always threatening to put a credit card machine by the front door of our house so our kids could swipe their cards as they came in and we could charge them for all the damage their kids did to our house when they left!

The following is a post of Don's that shows just what I am talking about. In true Don fashion, it captures the realness of what was happening, but he peppers it with a little humor:

> Friday, we all piled into our car and headed to the Oklahoma State Fair, which is a yearly tradition in our family. Carlie and Harison, our grandchildren, had a great time sliding down the slide with their parents, aunts, uncles, and grandmother (Lynda). We always eat fried cheese, roasted corn on the cob, corn dogs and other fair food. We enjoyed this evening with our family. I told them next year that we may have to break out the scooter.
>
> —Don

Carlie and Don going to the movies

Hutch, Emily and Don

Going on a walk with Hutch, Carter and Cooper

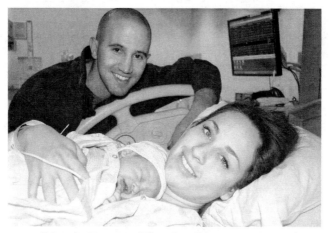

March 20, 2014 The day Olivia was born

6

The Odds and Ends of ALS

Because Don's ALS started in his foot, it progressed slowly for him, and we were able to maintain more of something that resembled a normal life (*normal* is a relative term here) for much longer than most. And for that, I will always be thankful (and we know Jonathan was too because of his awkward announcement at his only ALS support group!). When Don was first diagnosed, he was still working and running his landscaping company, and it was his hope that he could do that for as long as possible. At the same time, we knew that driving would be the first to go because the ALS started in his right foot. It was kind of a double-edged sword in that way; it meant it would spread more slowly, but it also meant that he'd lose control over that foot first and the other next, which would mean no more driving. We knew that would be a real hard blow to take because no more driving was kind of a marker for the first big loss of autonomy for him. That is one big thing I learned about ALS; as it attacks the body, it also slowly strips you of so many things you took for granted. It also makes you more and more dependent on others.

One by one, it takes things away—driving, walking, holding a spoon, brushing your teeth, going to the bathroom alone. And each one of these takes some time to come to terms with. It also puts a new task on the caregiver's list of things to do. For me, it was all a labor of love—every single moment of it. But I know Don felt like it was a burden for me. It could get tough, to be sure, but never in my life will I say or did I consider what I did for my husband a burden. I'd do it again a thousand times over. I'd do it day and night for the rest of my life if it meant I could have him back. But the fact is, I can't. I have to wait until I meet Saint Peter and God gives me the okay to see Don again. Until then, I want everyone to know as a caregiver, let your loved one with ALS know that you love them and that everything you do for them is out of love—not obligation or guilt or pity but *love*. Tell them that you're there with them and that things are tough but that they are always worth it—every second of every day.

My message to every caregiver out there is that I know, believe me I know, that it may be tough on us because we are doing so much, but think about your loved one who needs you there to brush his teeth or get her to the bathroom or change his clothes. It's hard—oh, is it hard—but be sure to let your loved one know that you'd do it until the end of time. Let them know that he or she is not a burden, that they are still the person you fell in love with. It's hard enough to lose the ability to eat by yourself; no one should feel ashamed or guilty that someone has to help them. I know Don felt like this at the end. I know because he'd apologize to me all the time. I couldn't imagine not being there. "Till death do us part"—I said it, and I meant it.

We were lucky enough that we got to ease into all the big changes. The disease wasn't painful in the first months, but Don was getting weaker in his right foot and leg as well as experiencing muscle spasms and tremors in both arms and legs. On the first vacation we took after the diagnosis, he got tired more quickly than before, and I noticed that he would drag his foot more as the day rolled on. He also told me that he just couldn't do some of the things he had always taken for granted—like being out running a landscaping company all day every day.

"I'm going to have to slow down more now and rest," he said, a little defeated. It's just another reminder of how unforgiving this disease can be. To tell the truth, I think we both got tired easier those days—Don because of the ALS and me because I always had so much on my mind, worrying about him and how he was taking all of it.

By July 2007, bigger changes took place around the Strahorn house. Ryan took over Don's business so Don could come home during the day and rest. Don went back and worked with his brother Tom for a short time until he just couldn't do it anymore. He also started wearing a brace on his right foot to help control his foot when he walked. It did help, but the brace made everything that much more real. At this point in our lives, all we could think about was how ALS was going to progress and in what way it would drastically change our lives. Don always worried about how long he would be able to work, drive, and get around without assistance. He had already had to step down from running the company. We couldn't help but wonder, *What's next?* And how long do we have until another piece is taken? We tried to make the best of it though. We enjoyed the time we had before the gadgets we knew were in our future and the loss of mobility. That is all we could do. With ALS, we learned to be prepared but to also keep focused on the moments that we had.

Eventually, Don had to get another leg brace for the left foot to help steady his legs that were getting weaker all the time. When those weren't helping anymore, he had to get two taller leg braces that went past his knees. The braces had to be made just for his legs for them to work like they should, so they were pretty pricey. To keep things lighthearted, after Don started wearing the leg braces, Jonathan decided he'd take it for a test drive. I think he had a new respect for his old man after that. They did not look easy to get around in!

Because Don was always the planner, we went ahead and got a wheelchair at a garage sale before he even needed it. We knew we'd have to get a nice one at some point, but we figured two chairs (a scooter and a wheelchair for a hundred dollars at a garage sale) would do the job for a while. Wheelchairs were anything but cheap, so we were holding off on buying one of the Cadillacs, as the man at the support group had described them. When it came time to get the motorized chairs, all the big boys took those out for a spin. We had a motorized wheelchair and a scooter, and Jonathan was determined to find out which one had more get-up-and-go. The girls respectfully declined the offer to race, so it was Clint who was left as Jonathan's competitor in the great wheelchair races of 2008. Because there would be no way to get a good feel for how fast the chairs were, naturally the boys had to race them down the street. Jonathan fared pretty well as a wheelchair racer; Clint, on the other hand, did more running into things than he did racing. His racing career was short-lived. And we all just prayed that Don would be better at maneuvering the chair when it came time for him to use them. If not, I figure we would need extra homeowner's insurance!

When Don finally couldn't walk anymore, it was time to retire the braces and move to the chair. We found out when Don got his Cadillac chair where Jonathan got his competitive spirit. One day when Harison was over, he and Don decided to race the two chairs down the street to see which chair was faster. To be sure that their findings were accurate, they had several races, and Harison won them all—in the old cheap garage sale chair!

"I let you win!" Don told Harison after his final defeat.

"No way! Why would you let me win, Papa?"

"I didn't want to damage the chair," he told him with a wink.

"I think it's because you drive the chair like you drive a car—SLOW!" I interjected.

One day I was out cleaning the garage, and all four braces were out there. When I found them, it struck me how odd they looked. They had seemed so normal for such a long time, but looking at them in the garage, I got a kind of uneasy feeling.

"Can I throw these away?" I asked Don, who was also watching me sifting through things.

"No," he said back, and I was surprised at how quickly and assuredly he responded.

"Why?" I protested. "You're not going to ever use them again."

He thought about it and said, "Nope, we're keeping them."

"What in the world are we going to do with them?" I insisted.

"Hmmmmm," Don said, studying the things, and then it hit him. "We will make lamps for each of the kids for Christmas!"

I just rolled my eyes. What else do you say to that?

I got a small taste of what Don must have been going through when I had to have two foot surgeries. I wasn't able to put any weight at all on one of my feet, so for two weeks, I adopted the old garage sale special wheelchair. Our living room looked like a parking lot for wheelchairs. I would have personally preferred the Cadillac, but Don said no way, so I got the old, shabby one. My chair had a speed control, but I am pretty certain there were only two speeds: "turtle" and "rabbit." Of course, I kept mine turned to rabbit. That was a little tricky because the chair also had a very sensitive joystick that controlled it. I found out how sensitive it was two days after my surgery when Don and I were watching a movie.

"Pause it," I said. "I need to go to the bathroom real quick." What a laugh! There was no "real quick" to anything I did at that point in time.

I had a time just maneuvering myself off the couch into that chair. It took me so long to get myself into the chair that I ran out of time to get myself to the bathroom. The second my backside hit the chair, I knocked that baby into rabbit speed to get me to the bathroom ASAP. I was off! I took off so fast I lost control and plowed right into the living room wall, knocking a sizable hole in the Sheetrock.

I didn't have time to care about a hole in the wall though. I looked over my shoulder at Don, who just sat in awe of his wife and her demolition job. I backed myself up and pulled forward, and I hobbled all the way to the toilet.

When I returned, I found my husband perched in front of my work, his phone up in the air focusing on it.

"I'm sending this to the kids!" he said as I stared at him now.

I read the text after he sent it: "Well look what your mom has done now…We are going to need to take out more insurance!" I couldn't help but think of Clint running into things that day they raced the wheelchairs and my little joke about how if Don were that bad at maneuvering a chair we'd need more home owner's insurance. As it turned out, I was the one we needed insurance for!

That two weeks in the wheelchair was such a pain for me. It made it hard to shower, get around, and make meals. I remember thinking about how I needed help for everything. I couldn't get comfortable in bed at night, I couldn't just get up and go to the other room, and I couldn't drive. I even had a hard time getting my pants on. This list goes on and on and on. I think the Lord used that experience to give me a tiny glimpse of what Don was going through. I had a light at the end of my tunnel; I knew I was going to heal, and I knew that I was going to walk again. But not my husband; he was only going to get worse.

Walking wasn't the only thing Don lost the ability to do that year. He also finally had to quit driving. He drove as long as he possibly could. We had moved to a handicap van by then because of the wheelchair. He was always one step ahead. As I watched his legs get weaker and weaker, I would ask again and again if it was time for him to quit driving. For a while, he was even driving with his left foot since the right was the first to go.

"Lynda Sue, I will let you know when I need to stop."

Then one day it happened. "I think it's time I quit driving," he told me.

What a defeat. It was just another thing he had to give up. It was so strange hearing those words. I knew they were coming. Shoot, I was the one asking him every other day if he shouldn't stop driving. But when he said those words, it was like someone had just punched me without provocation. I mean, a train may as well have crashed through my living room wall.

Now the real test to our marriage began—Don telling me how to drive! I'm going to be kind here and say that Don was a very cautious driver. So cautious I wanted to pull my hair out every time we went anywhere. I swear I may as well have gotten out and walked sometimes and I'd have gotten there faster. Everywhere he went, we were going the speed limit, if even that. This man was by the book now. He was one of those people who would drive in the slow lane get over just to pass someone and get right back in the slow lane. And he had the patience of a saint behind the wheel of a car. Me on the other hand, I drove like a race car driver. My pet peeve was staring at taillights. And the slow lane was a place that was a fairytale as far as I knew because I had never been there in my life. Don told me he was taking his life in his own hands getting in the car with me.

"You better watch out," I'd warn him. "I'll open that ramp door, make a hard left, and send you flying out if you keep on about my driving."

"Okay, but are you going to be able to pay that ticket when you get it?? he'd say at least one time every trip.

He learned to just shut his eyes (and his yapper) and wait to open them until we got to where we were going. That worked out best for everyone involved, I think. And I think I should say here, I never did get a ticket.

Two years into having ALS, we had lost seven friends from our support group. Seven. It was so hard to get to know these people and then watch them get so weak and fight with everything they had just to die. It was so heartbreaking knowing there was nothing anyone could do to change that. When you are talking about ALS, every year is huge because most patients only make it three to five years. Don and I were blessed that we had seven. And in those seven, we had five new grandchildren and one on the way. We were also blessed by the family and friends who were always there for us and a church family that was always praying for us. Don also had a slow progression of ALS, which doesn't happen very often. Even with all those blessings and so much to be thankful for, we always wondered if or when the disease would just take off. It was so scary not knowing what to expect. There were signs we could look for, but it was a very long waiting game all the time. It was like there was that boogeyman under the bed, always about to pop out and drag us under.

One thing the doctors really stressed was that I put as much weight on Don as I could because he would need it on him in the end. I did a great job at that, and I also put twenty-five pounds on myself! In the first year, one day Don found me hiding from him and sobbing. Don spotted me on the floor in our bedroom and patted me on the back, trying to calm me, and said, "Would it help if we went out to eat?" I guess he thought since I'd been eating like a horse with him that was what would make me feel better! On a serious note though, it was tough—the not knowing. And to know that it only got worse.

Everything that began to happen seemed like it could be life or death. In August 2009, a little over two years after Don was diagnosed, Don knew he wasn't feeling quite right. He would wake up in the middle of the night and move to the chair in the living room, just feeling odd; he said he just couldn't explain how he was feeling. One day he was out cleaning the windshield on the car, and he said that his upper body felt weak.

"I think it may be moving into my arms and chest," he said. My mouth went dry. I knew that was the beginning of the end. That wasn't the case that day, but the fear hung with me.

Another time in Florida, we had a similar scare. I went down to get a luggage cart for him to push, and it was too much for him. One day after lunch with Ryan and his brother Tom, he thought his chest and arms felt weak again. He just didn't feel right. Again, we thought it was the ALS moving. What we didn't know was that these were all signs that he was getting ready to have a heart attack! Tom rushed Don to the hospital that day after lunch. Some of the tests he took came back abnormal at first, but then when he took them again, they looked fine. They did some more tests to find out that he had 95 percent blockage in his main artery (the widow maker), with a blood clot ready to drop. The doctor said he was a ticking time bomb. They ended up putting in a stint to help because they couldn't do a bypass with the ALS. The doctor also couldn't use the medication he wanted because of ALS. Luckily, the stint did help him. We saw that situation in a glass half-full kind of way because it was a fixable heart problem, where we thought it was ALS spreading to a different part of his body. That was the crazy thing about ALS; you just never knew what it would do, so you thanked God for things like blockages and blood clots because those can be treated.

In the years Don battled ALS, we faced so many changes. It started with a walking cane, and I thought, *I can handle this*. Then it wasn't too long, and we had to get leg braces one leg at a time. We soon moved on to a walker and a breathing machine (noninvasive respirator). When he got too weak with the braces and walker, we moved on to a motor chair to help out with long distances; soon we needed it all the time. This chair meant we needed to get a handicap van.

In one year alone, we added a cheap wheelchair, handicap shower, urinal, cough assistant machine, shower chair, and slide boards to transfer from one chair to another. We even had to get special silverware for him to eat with.

The worst was probably the hospital bed and Hoyer lift. A hospital bed in your home only means one thing. Every day I had to face that one thing. Every day I was reminded of where all this was headed. It was one of the hardest days I had: the day I had to move out of our bedroom and across the hall so Don could sleep comfortably in the hospital bed. I remember it taking my breath away for the first few days when I would pass the room and glance in.

"Lynda, this isn't what you ever planned to have in our bedroom is it?" Don said when it arrived. It certainly wasn't.

Within the first week, I was out trying to find bedding for it. I don't mean just sheets; I wanted a comforter and pillow shams and throw pillows—anything to make it less like a hospital room and more like our home. I found a quilt and matching sheets and decided against the throw pillows; that was just silly. Every day when I got him out of bed, I would make that bed and do my best to make it look like a normal room. Some nights I would put Don into the bed, and he would ask me, "Could you just lay here with me for a few minutes?" I would squeeze my body on the edge of that twin-size hospital bed and lay my head on his chest. He would rub my head and back. We would talk about our life and kids. Sometimes I would doze off, and sometimes I would have to get up because it was so uncomfortable.

I would have to get up and go back across the hall and crawl into bed alone. There were many nights we would just talk back and forth across the hall like we were lying right next to one another. And there wasn't a night that he didn't say "I love you and thank you" from the other room. I just prayed and prayed he wouldn't ever lose the ability to talk. We may not have been in the same room, but we could at least still talk.

> Posted Feb 9, 2011 11:46am
> An update on what is going on at the Strahorn household. I have had a few changes since the last update with the progression of the ALS. I am using a power chair to get around now because my legs have become weaker causing a few falls. The grandkids are enjoying my new ride taking trips with me around the house and in and out of church. The ramp van has made a big difference being able to go places, being a back seat driver is not my strong suit but I am learning to be silent and just close my eyes as Lynda drives. There are days when I cannot button shirts and need help from Lynda to get dressed, these used to be the simplest tasks. Rolling over in bed and getting comfortable is becoming more difficult; also using a non-invasive respirator at night.
> These are the changes, but Lynda and I continue to feel so blessed with such a wonderful family, amazing friends and church family.

God continues to meet our needs and blessing our lives when you would think you could not feel peace, joy, strength in difficult circumstances, God is so good to us.

Now for the big news, Jonathan and Brandy will be married the first part of March and we will have our seventh grandchild in April as Jennifer and Jeremy will give birth to Avery Lynn Perry. Lynda and I are so excited about both events!

Love and Thanks

Don and Lynda Strahorn

Wheelchair races Harison and Don

Wheelchair race winner Harison with Hutch and Carter

Hutch and Don

Thanksgiving 2013 DewAnn, me, Tom, Don and Stacey

Jonathan and Brandy's wedding 2011

7

The Little Blessings that Come from the Pain

My family always loved doing things together. As time passed, more and more when we got together we tried to do things just for Don; we wanted to do the things we knew he enjoyed most. More often than not, for Don, that meant anything to do with golf. Jennifer took Don to the PGA championship practice round in Tulsa, and Clint, Ryan, and Jonathan called him to go golfing all the time. We were sure to recognize that as unlucky as being diagnosed with ALS was, we were lucky that it moves slowly and Don was able to play golf, even after he had the braces. If it wasn't the boys, he and our pastor would go with a small group of good friends. The doctors told him that it would be a good exercise for him. That was one order he didn't have to be persuaded to follow!

Golf was by far one of Don's favorite pastimes, although he would be the first to tell you he wasn't exactly going to be getting that green jacket anytime soon. He may have not been a pro, but golf was always something Don found fun and enjoyable. It wasn't just about the game either; it was about the people he played with.

"So, how'd ya play today?" I'd always ask when he'd come in after a day of golf.

"Well, I had a good time," he'd always respond.

"Bob beat you again?" I might tease. He'd just smile and shrug and repeat his mantra. "We had a good time."

Before Don was diagnosed with ALS, he would only get to golf every now and then when he could squeeze it in his schedule; but after his diagnosis, he made sure that he made time for it. (It was, after all, the doctor's orders!) Every invitation he got, he was there unless we had an important doctor's appointment or a family birthday. Don golfed as much as he could and with everyone he could. With ALS, there is no guarantee you'll be able to walk the coming month; so he squeezed in as much as he could, and he had a blast doing it. One Sunday, he, Ryan, and Jennifer went together; and when they got home, she said they just laughed the entire time. That is what they all needed at that time: laughter, quality time, and a little golf. That was September 2007. Later that night when Don and I talked, we realized that, at one point, we weren't even sure if he'd be able to walk by that time. It was a moment that we stopped to be thankful. Don had ALS, yes, but he was not only walking; he was out playing golf and laughing with his children. And for that, we thanked God!

Something else we found to be grateful for after the diagnosis was the patience and kindness of good friends. Don kept up his golf playing, even after he was using two leg braces, which was fantastic for him but could really slow a game down. His friends didn't mind at all though. They'd help him get his ball on the tee and drive him as close as they could to the hole, and several times they would even have to pick him up and get him back into a standing position after he would lose his balance and fall. Our great friend and pastor, Bob, was probably Don's closest golf companion. He has talked about those days out on the course with Don—about how Don would ask if he would tee his ball because if not, he would probably fall over at each tee box trying to do it. Bob talked about the great time they had together talking about golf, going down memory lane, and discussing what God had been doing in their lives. For Don and Bob both, the golf course was like a retreat from everyday life for them. And even with those little reminders of ALS—Don's weakening and being unable to bend down to put his ball on a tee—Don was never discouraged as he was having to ask for so much help, and our friends never got tired of helping. When he'd fall over, Don would just kind of chuckle at himself and keep on going. That was Don; he just kept on going and smiling and laughing and being grateful for all the joys we still had to be grateful for, and there were many. The following is a scripture that became near and dear to us, and I think it speaks volumes to anyone going through what we were:

> When those bitter days have come upon you far in the future, you will finally return to the Lord your God and listen to what he tells you. For the Lord your God is merciful— he will not abandon you or destroy you or forget the solemn covenant he made with your ancestors. (Deut. 4:30–31, NLT)

The Lord certainly did not abandon us, and Don was not going to live like he had, and so he kept on finding all the places of joy in his life. As silly as it may sound, the golf course was a place that kept hope going for him. It was something he could still do and do more of since he wasn't working all the time anymore. In a strange way, ALS helped slow him down to take up the things he wanted to do instead of the things he had to do. And during those times, we got quite a collection of stories. For instance, there was the time a squirrel snuck into Don and Ryan's golf cart and took off up a tree with Ryan's brand new bag of sunflower seeds. Don loved that one!

There is another golf memory of Don's that was bittersweet for all of us. He was with our friend Rod. They were on the eleventh hole, and Don had hit his second shot right into the green. The green was a bit of an incline— almost a small hill—so when Don went to putt, he had to stand with his heels toward the uphill part of the green. From the stories that have been told about this shot, everyone there looked at it and thought it was a pretty impossible shot. He was having a hard time standing, but he lined it up and took his swing. At that moment, he lost his balance and fell backward, right on his backside. And do you know what Don did? He broke out laughing, sitting there on his butt in the middle of the golf course, and Rod joined in.

This was the first time he had ever fallen while golfing. When I first heard the story, I remember thinking how amazing Don was; I think I might have cried if it would have been me. He did what he always did, however, and he made this disease easier for me and everyone around him to handle by not feeling sorry for himself and enjoying every day to the fullest, even when he was falling over on golf courses!

When they got home that day, they were still laughing about Don's little stumble. Of course, Don could hardly wait to tell me about it.

"Babe, you should have seen it. It was the funniest thing you'd ever seen. And after I fell, we heard the ball go in the hole!" he exclaimed, red from all the laughing he was doing. "I sunk the putt!"

"How did Don get up?" I asked.

"I had to pick him up!" Rod said, and they both laughed again!

The two decided that Tiger Woods would have been impressed with what Don pulled off that day on the course. And if you ask Rod about it, I think he'll tell you that God gave them that experience, which was funny and quite miraculous, as a time that he could always cherish—a great memory that Rod could hold on to.

I would hear endless stories of different putts, of long drives, and of all the fun Don was having out on the green. I would always listen and just smile, even though I wasn't quite sure what he was talking about 90 percent of the time.

As his disease progressed, I could tell how much weaker his legs were getting, and he would tell me that he didn't know how much longer he'd be able to play golf. I could tell this really bothered him. Golf had been one thing that helped him forget ALS and the future filled with wheelchairs and that he wouldn't watch any of his granddaughters walk down the aisle. To lose golf was more than just losing the ability to go out and play eighteen holes; he was losing something that was a way he connected with friends and family and something that made him who he was. The day he realized he couldn't play anymore had to be one of the darker moments in our journey. It was yet another thing that ALS was taking away!

Even after he was unable to play, Don still found ways to keep up his golf habit. Instead of playing, he'd watch. And instead of golfing, family and friends found other things to do with Don. And there was always the yard. Don had always taken care of it, and he continued to until he couldn't. After that, I took over yard duty, but Don would still be outside with me the entire time, giving his input (whether I wanted it or not) and just enjoying the smell of cut grass and the feel of the sun on his skin. As he continued to lose things, I began to make it a point to remember all the things he could still do. So we lost golf, but we still had eating, laughing, praying, and each other. And that was still a lot to be thankful for. As tough as it can be sometimes, this is something I found to be of great benefit, and I strongly suggest it to anyone else dealing with a terminal illness. As much as you can, count all your blessings and focus on what you still have rather than what you have lost. It's easy to lose sight of those things and take them for granted until they too are gone. So remember to recall all the things you still have and all the memories you are making that you can hold on to forever until you meet again.

Another bit of sunshine that came from the ALS diagnosis were the experiences we had doing fund-raisers and raising awareness for ALS. One of the fund-raisers was a golf tournament we did in 2012. That was certainly a highlight of the year. We were raising awareness with Don's favorite sport. We also did an ALS walk at the Oklahoma City Zoo. The donations that were received went to flu shots, research, support groups, and helping patients get those expensive wheelchairs. And of course, there were the 4Don@Dusk fun runs that always reminded us of how blessed we were, even in the hardest of times.

The following is a post from Don that I think is particularly poignant. It is a kind of reflection about a year and a half into the diagnosis. I love it because it shares his side of things instead of just mine.

Posted Aug 25, 2008 9:26pm

I'm sorry that we have not updated the CarePage recently, but everything is going well. My health has not changed much since my last doctor's visit and my next appointment is September 11th. Our family is looking forward to going to the lake the first part of September. Our annual trip to the State Fair of Oklahoma is this month, where we will go and eat our favorite food (which is not healthy but sure tastes good once a year) and visit a few exhibits.

Last year we went to the MDA telethon for the first time and are looking forward to attending this year. This year Lynda and I and possibly a few of the kids will do an interview about ALS and about how the MDA has impacted our lives. This will air between 9:30 to 10:00 Monday morning. I had the opportunity to share with our church this past Sunday about how MDA and ALS has and will impact our lives. I would like to share with you what I shared with them.

March 27, 2007, I was diagnosed with ALS, more commonly known as Lou Gehrig's Disease. That day was when we became involved with the MDA, and they have been there every step of the way. Helping us cope with, understand what to expect, and helping meet our needs as they arise. This has been done through monthly support group meetings, where MDA representatives, a psychologist, and families dealing with ALS all share experiences, joys, and trials of what each of us is dealing with. We have not yet experienced a portion of most, but are greatly appreciative of each person sharing their lives with us. The MDA also helps defray cost of clinical visits, equipment purchases which includes wheelchairs, braces, communication devices, and other equipment. There is also a loan closet where individuals in need of or waiting for equipment to be delivered can use at no cost.

Research is a large part of the MDA. ALS is one of over 43 diseases that falls under the umbrella of the MDA, of which there is no treatment or cure yet. Before all of this happened I had heard of Lou Gehrig's Disease but did not understand what was involved. I am one of approximately 200 people in Oklahoma, and 30,000 people nationally that has ALS, with approximately 5,000 being diagnosed annually. These numbers do not change drastically because once a person is diagnosed their life expectancy is 2 to 5 years with only 10% living ten years or longer. What happens are the nerve cells in the brain and spinal cord that control voluntary muscle movement start to die. As this happens this affects everything that a person does.

We are hopeful that this year there will a major breakthrough in the research for a cure for these diseases. I regret not telling in more detail of the affects of ALS, but I could feel that my emotions were changing as I was pretty nervous to begin with speaking before a large group. I also wanted to say that how appreciative we are for everyone's support and prayers for our family and that our strength, joy and peace come from and through our relationship with our Lord and Savior Jesus Christ.

Thanks and Love from the Strahorn Family.

Don Strahorn

Don, Jennifer, and I went to an MDA telethon for a few hours to see what it was all about a couple of years in. We all saw some bits and pieces of TV every year, but we never dreamed that we would be a part of it someday, or why.

"I guess I'm one of Jerry's kids now!" Don said as we strolled around the place.

I was amazed to see how many people were involved and how hard they worked for the people in need. The year that we went to the telethon, Oklahoma raised 1.4 million dollars and nationwide they raised 61 million dollars! To this day I hold out hope that they will continue to raise money so that they will find a cure and no one will need to read my book again, unless they just like to hear funny stories about a quirky family who happened to lose an amazing man. That is another reason that I write this book. I want more and more people to become aware and to get involved too. You don't have to have ALS or a loved one with it to get involved. And the MDA is a great place to start as they help a number of people with a number of diseases, as Don's post above explains.

We became warriors against ALS, which I think helped us feel more empowered against the disease once Don was diagnosed. One year Don was even the ALS representative for the state of Oklahoma. We even got to meet with Governor Brad Henry. Don, Jennifer, and I went to the state capital and met the governor. We met him in May, ALS awareness month. Governor Henry had just signed a proclamation making May ALS Awareness Month to increase the public's awareness of the impact this devastating disease has, not only on the person living with ALS but also on his or her family and friends. It was also to raise awareness to keep critical research underway to eradicate ALS.

We learned at our various ALS functions that approximately two hundred Oklahomans have ALS; five thousand people are diagnosed annually, and there are an estimated thirty thousand cases nationally. With a small percentage of people affected, it does not get the attention that other diseases and illnesses may. Don had the opportunity to share our story that May through the media to try to inform the public about the effects of this disease and to explain that it does not discriminate. Anyone can be diagnosed with ALS at any time. And if that time comes, there is no cure as of right now. Don was working to change that, and I will continue to do the same.

The day Don met the governor and shared our personal story with the state, someone asked what treatment he was receiving for the disease. This may have been the most eye-opening moment of the event.

"Well, there is no treatment and still no known cause or cure for this disease," he explained.

That was a pretty sobering statement from Don, but what was amazing about it is that he was able to make it. Don was able to act as a representative for a disease that is often overlooked, and for that, we were also thankful.

There were so many things to be thankful for the seven years we lived with ALS. That we got seven years was a miracle itself. But I hope if this chapter leaves you with anything, it is the knowledge and hope that there is a way to find great moments of happiness even after the devastation of a terminal disease comes in and wrecks everything you had planned. There will always be hard times, and knowing that a loved one only has a small amount of time is never going to be easy, but there can be little hidden blessings that come to us in times of pain. We just have to be sure we are looking for them and that we aren't so focused on the pain that they pass us by.

After Don was diagnosed, we appreciated every second, and we also made our time count. Most importantly, we learned to do things that bring us happiness instead of letting the daily grind swallow us whole. That was a blessing, and it made the last seven years I had with my husband the most amazing and love-filled seven years of my life.

Don and Ryan Golfing

Don

Golf Tournament fund raiser for Don. Steve,
Don and Bob (our Pastor and friend)

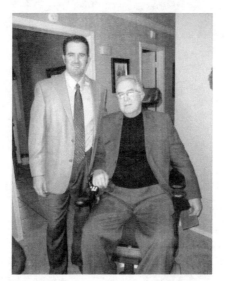

Don and Ryan going to an ALS event

Dinner with friends 2012 Steve, Fran, Kathy and Alan

8

Dirty Jobs: The Nitty-Gritty of Living with ALS

The August after he was diagnosed, Don fell down for his first time. That set off little alarms in my head. I knew that was just one of many to come (I already discussed his golf course incident). When it happened, he had said he had been feeling less stable, so in a way we knew it was coming. But that is how ALS works; you know it's coming, but still it is jarring and unsettling, not to mention heartbreaking. We both knew what it meant when he started to fall—that he was losing his mobility, and soon walking would be out of the picture. Mark another thing off the list.

The doctor's big concern at that point was about him getting hurt during a fall. If Don were to break something, he would never regain that muscle; so I had to be sure we kept him off the floor and on his feet! And I will tell you this, as time passed, that got harder and harder to do. Don stayed optimistic, of course, but I know that the idea of not walking at all was tough for him. Still, we remained grateful that it was progressing slowly, even if we did have to prepare for the inevitable. We talked a lot about what lay ahead of us and how we would handle it. And we just prayed all the time that the disease would keep on moving slowly. Of course, we also prayed for a cure or some kind of miracle.

As the contractors worked on our bathrooms throughout the fall of 2007, Don started to get weak in his other leg, which meant two braces instead of one. With a second brace and more weakness, we all saw a decrease in speed and energy in Don. Every little decrease was like the loss of ground for us. That is how it worked; it's like a melting ice cube in a way. Little by little, more melts away that can never come back. What is so hard with ALS is that you can't do anything about it. There was no freezer for us to get to stop the melting. All you can do is sit by and watch. So we all watched as Don got weaker and more unstable. And to keep from getting swept up in gloom, we stayed happy that his arms were still good and his speech was impeccable. We had to hang on to the part of the ice cube that was still there, and we did. Don was breathing well and able to eat without any problems, even if he did wear out faster.

It took a couple of years for Don to move into a wheelchair full time. There were two years of stumbling, catching himself, losing the ability to get up and down stairs or to make it far without resting, and of course falling, and it happened more and more until the day finally arrived. We had to put up the braces and move to the chair. That came with a handicap van, ramps, and a bathroom remodel, just to be able to get around. (A quick note: all those things good friends helped us get; I cannot thank our friends enough for all they did at that time.) As hard as it was, how grateful I was and am that we had that amount of time. Like I said before, some people passed within a couple of years of diagnosis, so Don moving into a wheelchair was a miracle in and of itself. But it was about this time that he also started noticing weakness and twitching in his shoulders and arms. That, we knew, would be a whole other ball game. Not being able to walk or golf or work in the yard anymore, which was what was slowly happening, was one thing. But when Don lost the strength is his arms, that would mean the loss of really basic things—things that we don't just take for granted but feel like if we can't do them, we are losing our autonomy in a major way. Eating, brushing your teeth, shaving, going to the bathroom—these are the things that would slip from Don's grasp next, quite literally. And that really did change everything. As I watched Don slowly deteriorate, I would sit back and realize that it all felt so surreal. Even after years into the diagnosis, it was still hard to believe that it was happening to our family. But then something would happen—a fall or a new brace or the need to move full time into a wheelchair, and there was no getting around the fact: this was *real*.

At a support group meeting one night after Don was in his wheelchair, a woman whose husband has ALS said, "We as caregivers are grieving every day." I never thought about it that way, but it hit me right then that she was right. With each fall or twitch or loss with Don, I hit a new grieving process. The disease was hard on everyone. It was always stealing something, but I knew it couldn't take what we had in the Lord. Even as horrible as it was, we knew we were still so blessed, and I would not have changed my life for another. We relied on the following prayer constantly to remind us of what we had:

> The man who patiently endures the temptations and trials that come to him is the truly happy man. For once his testing is complete he will receive the crown of life which the Lord has promised to all who love him. (James 1:12)

There are some things with ALS that no amount of prayer can save you from, and that is when you use prayer to help you get through it since there is no avoiding it. Strangely, some of these things helped to distract us from the bigger picture, and that was a peculiar comfort—a very peculiar comfort. Let me explain what I mean.

One night around midnight, Don woke up and had to go to the bathroom, so I got up to help him. This meant I lifted him from his wheelchair to the toilet. I went back and lay down and waited until he called me back so I could lift him back to the chair and then get him back in bed. That night, his call back was a little different,

"Lynda! Lynda! I need help! Hurry!" he called out to me.

When I heard him, I ran to the bathroom. When I got to the door, I saw him sprawled out on the floor. He had fallen off the toilet. He was a jumbled up mess on the floor, and his legs were hurting because of it.

"Help me up!" he panted as I tried to figure out how in the world I was going to get him off the floor.

I wedged my arms beneath him and heaved as hard as I could to get him up. Nothing. He was too low for me to get him to the chair. I knew if we went at it like that for too long I'd throw my back out and we'd both be stuck on the floor. I pulled him out so he was at least lying straight on the floor. At that point, half of him was in the bathroom, and the other half was in the bedroom. I might mention he was stark naked and face down!

He turned and looked up at me, and I said, "Well, what are we going to do now?"

"Don, just let me think a minute!" I snapped back, shushing him as I thought about what we would do. "Let's call Jonathan!" I finally said, and then I threw a blanket over him.

"What in the world are you doing?" he asked as the blanket settled over him.

"Well, you just look so cold," I replied. I don't know why, but I couldn't stand for him to be laid out without at least a blanket. He just shook his head.

I called Jonathan, and he came right over; that's what firemen do. When he got to the bedroom door, he stopped and looked at Don.

"This is a familiar scene," he said, studying his father. Firemen get called on assisted lifts all the time. But this time, it was his dad. "What's up with the blanket?" he asked, cocking his head to the side.

"Your mom thought I looked cold!" Don blurted.

Jon had no problem getting Don back into his bed. I thanked him and headed to bed myself, glad we had gotten through that. But the next one would be even worse!

Another night at about the same time as our last incident, I heard Don calling me to take him to the bathroom. I stumbled into the room, half-asleep.

"You need to hurry, babe," he told me with a sense of urgency I couldn't miss. I hurried to get him into his chair, which was quite a process. I had to raise him up then swing his legs around. Then I had to move his chair up while I was still holding him so he didn't fall backward. I put my arms under his arms and around him and then hoisted him to his chair. In my head, I would count to three every time before I lifted him. He made the comment "I'm proud I married a stout woman" one time as I went through all this to get him into the shower.

"Next time you call me a stout woman I will drop you flat on your butt!" I warned him. So he decided to tell that to all our friends instead of me. I heard him say that so many times: "I am glad I married a stout woman!" Luckily for him, I didn't keep my promise! And let me tell you, I wanted to this one particular night.

I worked as fast as I could to get him to the bathroom, but I didn't get him there fast enough. Before I could get him out of his chair, it was too late, if you catch my drift. The moment it happened, we both just stopped. I stepped back and looked at Don. I was mad at myself, I was mad at him, and most of all, I was tired! I collapsed onto his bed that I was standing beside and just sat silently.

"We should probably—"

"Hush," I said, holding a hand up to stop him. "I just need to think a minute."

In that moment, I felt so sorry for him and for me. I was exhausted, and I knew he was too. And there we were, in a bedroom that was only getting less aromatic by the second. There was a giant mess to clean, and I didn't even know where to start. Why? Why? Why? Why? That's all I could think for a moment, but I finally pulled myself together, slapped on some gloves and a mask, got him out of the chair, and started cleaning. After I got the mess cleaned up, it occurred to me I needed to get *him* cleaned up. So at 1:30 a.m., I called Ryan to come help me get him into the shower. I met Ryan at the front door with my mask and gloves on, holding a set of each for him!

"Is that really necessary, Mom?" he asked looking at the gear I offered him.

"You're gonna want them, believe me," I said, pushing the gloves and mask at him.

"I am so sorry, guys," Don said again and again that night. "I am so embarrassed."

"Cut it out," I told him. "You don't need to say sorry. But don't let it happen again," I added with a wink. The strange thing was, this was not something that was ALS-related. With ALS, you don't lose control of your bowels. We just weren't fast enough that night! I never imagined this happening, since bowel control wasn't an issue, but it happened nonetheless—another little surprise from ALS! There are some ancillary incidents that come with a disease like this. So I guess what I'm saying is, expect anything!

After that, Don would often make sneaky calls from the toilet. I would go on with whatever I needed to do once I got him there, and he would call Ryan and whisper, "Hey, could you come down here and help Mom and get me off here and help put me in bed tonight?"

I'd catch him on occasion, at which time Don and Ryan both would hear me bellowing from the kitchen or living room, "Don! Are you calling Ryan again?! I can do it. Leave him alone!"

Don was always worried about me getting hurt trying to help him, so anytime he thought he could, he would ask the boys to come help. I think he also called the boys just to get them there. They had a wonderful special bond that only a father and sons could have. In all his random late-night calls, not once did either Ryan or Jon not answer or say they couldn't do it.

As the ALS moved along, slowly but surely, Don lost big and little things. There was going to the bathroom and showering that he needed assistance with, but he also started having a hard time trimming his own fingernails. He also got to the point that he needed me to brush his teeth and eventually help with what he ate. We realized brushing teeth was a job that needed to be outsourced when I found Don's head in the sink. He was in his wheelchair and was trying to brush his teeth, and his arms got so weak that he slowly fell over into the sink and couldn't push himself back up. I heard a muffled shout coming from the bathroom and had no idea what was going on. When I got to him, Don's head was buried in the sink. I grabbed him by the back of the shirt and pulled him up.

"What in the world are you doing?" I asked.

"Thank God the water wasn't on!" he said when I got him resituated. "I could've drowned in my own sink!"

We decided it was time I take over the task. The first time I brushed his teeth with his electric toothbrush, I forgot to put it in his mouth before I turned it on. Toothpaste splattered the walls and both of us. You'd think from so much practice brushing my own teeth I'd be fine, but when you do something for others, it's like you're a kid learning how to do things all over again.

The following is a post from Don that gives a little insight to what it felt like for him as he slowly lost the most basic of abilities:

> Posted Feb 6, 2012 5:56pm
>
> Just relaxing in my recliner as I do most days thinking about Carter and Hutch spending the night with us the other night.
>
> Hutch enjoys staying the night but this was a big deal for Carter because he would rather be in his own bed to sleep.
>
> It was such nice weather Lynda decided to cook steak for dinner which sounded good to me. Dinner time, we are all at the table and I look at our plates and the steak has been cut in small pieces not only for the boys but also for me. (I do appreciate this) Lynda has already promised the boys pancakes and bacon for breakfast the next morning.
>
> The boys are up early eating and now it is time for Lynda to get them dressed for the day. I looked down the hall and said when you get done would you come help me get dressed. My life is following the boys lives a lot lately, I am glad they're already out of diapers! We can find humor in a lot these days.
>
> —Don Strahorn

Don wasn't the only one doing comical things those days. One Sunday morning, we were running late for church. I hurried around in getting Don and myself ready. We got to the front door, and I stood in front of him ready to open the door. When I opened it, he just sat there. I wondered why he wasn't going, but finally he explained.

"Are you ready for church?"

"Yes. Why?" I asked.

"You sure?" he asked, and his eyes dropped to my bottom half. I followed his glance and realized that there I stood in my shirt, slip, and shoes! I had forgotten to put on my skirt! Yet again, one of those little things you don't think of. It is all too easy to forget to take care of yourself when you are taking care of a loved one with something like ALS. All your duties are doubled, and it is easy to get lost in the mix. Thankfully, Don was there to catch me in the moments I needed him to.

It got to the point that I needed help, and not just calling on Ryan and Jonathan in the middle of the night. At that point, we went to hospice, which is another one of those "Is this happening?" moments because the first thing you think of when you think of hospice is death.

As leery as I was about hospice, we were so fortunate to get the most amazing two women to care for Don. One of the women was his nurse and the other was a younger woman, and both were as sweet as they come. Don was sure to let me know that the nurses' aid was much gentler when she bathed him.

"Yeah?" I replied when he told me. "Well, I get you cleaner!"

"You really are lacking gentleness in the fruits of the spirit, Lynda Sue," he reminded me. I could think of a few more I was lacking in as he critiqued my bathing strategies: also patience and self-control!

When I first thought of Don having to be bathed by a young woman, I thought he'd be mortified. I was so relieved to see that it got easier with time. Of course, it wasn't ideal, but it wasn't as awful as I had expected. She would come three days a week to bathe Don, and I would shower him the other days. She would also do any oral hygiene and stripped his sheets. The first day she came, I could see how uncomfortable Don was; I was too. I felt so sorry for him because I knew he was nervous, but he handled it like a pro. Every time she came, it seemed to get easier. I always stayed out of the room because I thought it would make it more uncomfortable for all of us. To make it easier on him, the aid had Don clean his unmentionables, and I'm not talking about underwear because Don got rid of those since he was in a wheelchair and didn't need them anymore. He offered them to our boys one day, and they kindly declined; I have to say the looks on their faces were priceless when he asked. One day, Don lost the soap while the nurse was showering him. This caused a bit of a problem.

"I had a little incident in the shower today!" he told me when she was gone.

I couldn't imagine what a little incident with another woman in the shower could be! This was not your usual marital conversation. At that point, his grip was weak, and he had trouble holding things. This is what caused the fiasco.

"While I was cleaning my private areas, the soap slipped out of my hand and went up under my leg, and I couldn't find it! I had to ask her if she would get the soap back for me! So she had to dig the soap from, well, you know."

I almost bust a gut from laughing so hard. I never imagined I'd be laughing at my husband telling me a woman rooted around in his business in the shower, but ALS has a way of bringing about the most unusual of circumstances. The first thing I did was send a message to all our kids. Nothing is private or off-limits when you're dealing with a disease. The girls thought it was as funny as I did, but the boys were mortified. I also told a few friends, who brought Don his very own specially made soap on a rope. The rope was just long enough that it couldn't get lost and could be retrieved!

There were also the machines that come with the disease and the strangeness of sleeping in different rooms, which I've mentioned a little. One night I woke up, and I couldn't hear Don's breathing machine. It had become a noise I depended on—one that was a fixture in our house and let me know Don was still breathing. There were so many sounds I had come accustomed to: the sound of him moving in his hospital bed, his noninvasive ventilator, him turning his light on and off. Subconsciously, I think I listened for the sounds all the time. That night, I couldn't hear the machine. I lay there for a few minutes thinking about how quiet it was, and then I panicked. I jumped up and rushed to his room, terrified of what I might find. I didn't turn any lights on. I just leaned over Don to see if I could hear him breathing. All of a sudden, his eyes opened, and I could see a smile pop up on his face.

"Gotcha!" he said. "You making sure I'm breathing?"

"Dang it, Don!" I said as I whacked him in the chest. Nothing like a good joke in the middle of the night!

By the seventh year after Don was diagnosed with ALS, things were changing daily it seemed. We were on borrowed time by then, according to the stats. Don had lost the use of his legs and hips, and it was moving to his arms, hands, chest, and back. He started to want to stay home a lot more because it was just easier than getting ready and getting out. Don had also lost all the weight I put on him and then some.

His breathing was also getting weaker. It was around that time Don made the choice not to get a feeding tube. When you start to make those decisions and hospice is in your house three days a week, you all know what is coming. As much as we wanted to look the other way, it was right there, staring us in the face.

Jonathan and Don at the fire station

Thanksgiving 2013 Jennifer and Don

Thanksgiving 2013 Jaclyn and Don

9

Preparing for the Unthinkable

We would go to support group meeting on the second Tuesday of each month. Where we first dreaded them, we had begun to look forward to going and seeing our new friends; we called them *pals*. But about a year in, I remember a particularly hard night. Someone visited the group to talk about life support and being ready to make that decision when the time came. I knew that these were things we needed to be ready for, and Don and I always talked about them; but sitting there in that meeting and looking around at the sweet faces of our new friends just broke my heart. Some of them were going so fast; many were going to have to make the life support decision soon, and we both knew it. There were also those people moving to hospice all the time. Don would sometimes say that he felt guilty that his was moving so slowly. While my heart broke for our pals, I thanked God all the time for Don's slow-progressing

ALS. In my heart, I just knew that the Lord had a plan for Don. Even knowing that though, we couldn't ignore all the signs that showed us what was inevitable. One of the worst was when we lost Susan, who we had met at our very first meeting and had an instant connection. She was two years older than Don and was diagnosed a week before him. At that meeting, she won my heart as soon as she spoke. She was giving God the glory for all things, but she so desperately wanted a miracle. During the meeting when Don started to speak, he began to cry; she went straight to him with a tissue. She felt his pain. At the end of the meeting, she came to me and hugged me with a hug like I have never had before. She had so much love for life and for those around her, but mostly for her Lord Jesus.

The last year of her life, we watched her sweet daughter bring her mother to the meetings and other events for ALS. She would take care of her and help us understand what she was saying as her speech got worse. We watched as Susan lost her ability to speak, use her arms and hands, eat, and walk, but not her ability to love. I still had so many things to say to her about the impression she had made on our lives, but just like that, she was gone. Susan didn't get the miracle she was asking for in this life. And her death reminded me of how fast an ALS patient could be gone. It was just terrifying.

As time passed, Don became weaker. First his legs went, and then it started in his arms. It was when his breathing numbers started to go down that we knew we had to really prepare. His lungs had always been at 100 percent, but that started to slip too. Then there were the cramps all over his body, and the way the smallest things would keep him in bed for a week or more. Every little sign became a big sign. And it became harder and harder to see the humor in it all. We tried to still, but it was just getting harder every year. Then in March of 2013, we hit an obstacle that we all knew was a bad omen. Don got pneumonia, which made him weaker than ever. And when you have ALS, any muscle you lose is never coming back.

We had a rough and scary March, but he fought through it with family, friends, and hospice by his side. Although hospice was yet another reminder of what was to come, they were a true godsend throughout the month of March, there for all of Don's needs.

Even after he recovered from pneumonia, Don was getting out less and less. He even started listening to the church service every week on the computer instead of going to church. Going to family events became so taxing for him, and if we did go, we could never stay too long because they wore him out. They took everything he had. What others could do on a whim, like packing up and going to a relative's, it took us hours to prepare for and felt like running a marathon to Don. It was around this time that he also started to drastically drop weight. When the doctors noticed the rapid weight loss, yet another ugly monster reared its head.

"Don, at this point, we need to know if you'd like a feeding tube."

"I don't," he told the doctors. Don had already told the family this, and as a family, we all decided that we were there to support him in all his wishes.

By then, Ryan and Jonathan were at the house every night to help me get him into bed or to lift him to get him from one place to another. Jennifer and Jaclyn helped with clipping nails and cutting his hair. It took the entire family, as Don was losing more and more function all the time. He couldn't move his legs or feet, write his name, unlock a door, open a can, shave, clip his nails, shower himself, open the toothpaste, get a fly off his leg, comb his hair, hold a phone to his ear, or put his shirt on. And the list just continued to grow. We just prayed that it wouldn't move to eating or speaking. How we prayed. As we marked one thing after the next off the list, we prayed and prayed.

Don's right lung soon lost all function, and only the top of his left lung was working, which made breathing a chore. It also made speaking harder to do for him. At this time, his tailbone also started to throb. Being stuck in a wheelchair or a bed and having no muscle put a lot of strain on Don's tailbone, and there was not much to do about it since he had no use of his legs or arms. That was another injustice of

ALS; you can't move, but you can still feel. So the function is gone, but the pain is not.

With Don getting weaker, we had to be overly cautious about germs, not an easy thing to do with so many grandkids. As all this was going on, Jennifer and her family moved to Tulsa. The day she left, she gave Don a hug good-bye, and they both started crying. The whole room was in tears. We were all completely aware of the fact that every moment had become more precious than ever as the disease spread. Not long after Jennifer left, Don started having trouble breathing like he never had before. It was November by then. We were in the living room watching a movie when it happened. As soon as I realized what was going on, I hurried to get him in bed and on his respirator. I gave him his meds, hoping they would help; and eventually they did a bit, but we knew that it was just a Band-Aid on a severed limb. I spent that night listening for his breathing. The next day, I called our nurse from hospice, and she had some meds sent out for him to help him get through it if it happened again. About a week and a half later, it did. I gave him the meds, and they seemed to relax him. I don't know if it did me though. Every time got scarier.

We knew that the loss of lung capacity was the beginning of the end. It was so heartbreaking. And now, we couldn't even escape the house to get our minds off it. We were tethered to medications and breathing machines. All the things we had feared were coming to pass. Because of that,

Don began to work to complete his bucket list. Instead of places to visit or things to do, it was things he wanted done for me so I wouldn't have to worry about it when he could no longer take care of it—things like having our fireplace fixed, our air conditioner replaced, trees trimmed, a tree planted, financial advice, cleaning out files, and so on. He walked me through taxes, bills, and so many things that I could hardly keep them sorted out. Like I said, Don was a planner. And as much as I hated having to do it because of what it meant, it was necessary. Because of Don's planning, we were at least as ready as we could be. This is something that is very difficult, but I urge everyone to do it. Sit down and make sure everything is straightened out. The last thing you want as you grieve the loss of a loved one is to try to figure out what is going on with finances and where the tax information is filed. Don made sure that I could make it on my own, even if I was convinced I never could.

As Don got weaker, it got harder to move him, and I was more grateful for hospice than ever before. Not only did they help move him but they were also there with advice on how to cope and manage each day and the new needs that came with the progression. Even as we prepared for the worst, Don faced each day as he had throughout the seven years with strength, integrity, prayer, and love for others. The farther along it got, the more you could see that he truly was one special man!

What I noticed those last months was that it seemed like every time someone called, texted, emailed, or came by, they always wanted to know how Don was, but the next question was "And, Lynda, how are you doing?" My answer to that most of the time was "Okay," but really what I was thinking was "I don't get out and go anywhere much anymore, and if I do, it is very quickly because I'm afraid not to be home with Don." That is how it is at the end. Every second away, all you can do is hurry to get back because *what if?* What if he needs you? Or takes his last breath and you aren't there? What if he calls out for you and you don't come? What if?

When I did get out alone, it all came closing in on me, and I'd start crying. It was when I was alone that I had time to think of something other than what Don needed in that moment, and then I was bombarded with emotions. Taking care of Don was not just my way of serving Jesus; it was what kept my mind busy. I had a friend who lost her husband tell me that she felt it was an honor and privilege that God chose her to care for him at the end of his life, and that is exactly how I felt. So the answer to how I was doing then is, I was sad, scared, tired, but I felt love like I never felt before, and I felt blessed with a wonderful husband, children, family, and friends. But while I felt blessed, every day Don would apologize to me for needing so much from me. He would apologize for the things I had to do for him and the future that we would not have. And all I could say to him was he would do the same for me a million times over!

When we said our wedding vows thirty-six years before, I never knew how the words we said to each other would have so much meaning to me until those final days. "To have and to hold from this day forward, for better or for worse, for richer, for poorer, in sickness and in health, to love and to cherish; until death do us part."

> Trust in Him at all times, O people; pour out your hearts to him, for God is our refuge. (Ps. 62:8)

On one visit, the hospice nurse noticed that Don started to cry as they talked. She asked Don if he felt like he needed some antidepressants. He said if she thought he did, then maybe, so she ordered them for him. The next day, Don said to me after he had only taken one of the pills, "I'm not taking these. I'm not depressed. I was just sad yesterday." That is another thing; sometimes you are just plain sad. Who wouldn't be? But what you have to keep in mind is that God is there, and you have been given the gift of that person you are caring for. And although those final times are so, so hard, you have to remember the countless memories you have made and all the times you did have because there could have been so many fewer.

Don and me at the zoo 2013

Don and Carter

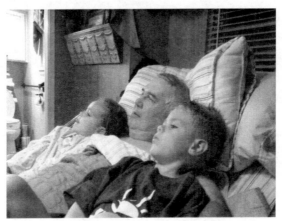

Emily, Don and Hutch

10

The Final Days: The Hardest Good-bye

The month of December Don was getting much weaker and losing weight faster than I ever thought a person could. He was still able to eat, but he only ate tiny amounts at a time. By this time, he had everything in order because we knew it was coming. He even had Jennifer help him order a camera for me and a beautiful birthstone ring with both our birthstones in the setting. It was near Christmas, and he wanted to be sure that if it did happen, I would still have gifts from him to open. He never quit thinking of me—ever.

We watched a lot of Hallmark Christmas movies at that time. These made for a lot of emotional evenings. On one night, one of the movies focused on the passing of a loved one. I couldn't keep the tears from coming, but I tried to hide them from Don. When I looked over at him, I saw that he was also sobbing. I got up and went to him. And together, we let the tears go.

"I don't want to leave you and the kids," he told me over his tears. "I love you all so much."

That was a breaking point in so many ways. I didn't want him to leave us either. But I also knew that he was so tired, so weak. He was ready to leave his body that was of no use to him anymore. But his heart and mind were so clear and healthy. The two were in entirely different places, which made it all that much harder. Don was so torn; he was ready to be with his Lord, but he wasn't ready to leave us. I can tell you that we weren't ready either, not by a long shot. He had no idea how much we were going to miss him. That wasn't something I could say though. Telling someone you don't know how you'll go on without them doesn't make their dying any easier. Because the fact was, no matter what any of us wanted, Don's body was giving out.

We made it through Christmas, and it was a particularly poignant Christmas that year. Nothing could be more bittersweet than knowing it was the last time you'd ever unwrap presents with the man you had loved for four decades. Everything was so emotional. It was the last time Don would tell his grandchildren "Merry Christmas!" and the last time I'd get a gift that he had picked out. I tried to focus on all the good things though so I wouldn't be swallowed whole by sadness. Don was so weak on Christmas, but he was there, and so we all were sure to cherish that.

As Don read his Bible that morning, his scripture was Isaiah 41:10: "Don't be afraid, for I am with you. Do not be dismayed, for I am your God. I will strengthen you. I will help you. I will uphold you with my victorious right hand." This scripture carried him through the next four days to his birthday on New Year's Eve. That year, he turned fifty-seven years old. The day that we celebrated another year of life for Don was so strange because it was that day that things really started to decline. He had been using morphine drops the past few months for pain when he had trouble breathing. He could usually tell when he would need them. But that day, everything changed.

We had had a fairly quiet day; some friends had brought a pizza over for Don's birthday. When they left, I fixed him a piece. He tried to eat it but stopped and asked me to take him to the bathroom. I did and then left to give him privacy for a couple of minutes. When I stepped back in, I could see something was wrong. He looked panicked.

"Please get me off here!" he said, his voice strained but frenzied. I moved him as quickly as I could. I had no idea what was happening, but his expression sent waves of panic in me too. "I think I just took my last breath," he said, his voice was no more than a whisper.

I rushed to get him his medication, but nothing seemed to help. I called Ryan, and he rushed over. When Ryan got there, Don and I were both crying. I remember how scared Ryan looked when he walked in. I think we all were. The moment we had all been pushing out of our minds but that had haunted us since the diagnosis was rapidly approaching.

Calls went into the hospice nurse, the doctor, our pastor, and the rest of the kids. The doctor changed his morphine to every four hours to keep Don from being what he called "air hungry," and he wasn't, but it took a bit of time to get there. Even with his breathing back, Don was scared. All the lightheartedness that usually filled our house, and him, had kind of drifted away. It had disappeared in the knowledge of what was to come. Ryan sat on the couch with his head buried in his hands, and I was in a chair sobbing. When Pastor Bob arrived, even their interactions were different. His eyes filled with tears as he sat with his golfing buddy.

"I never thought I was a weak man, but I don't think I can do this anymore…I couldn't breathe," Don said, his voice still barely sneaking out.

"There's nothing weak about you," Bob told him. "You are the strongest man I know."

At that point, we prayed that the Lord would take him quickly and that he wouldn't suffer anymore. Then the meds started to kick in, and things started to calm down. When Ryan and I put him in bed that night, he told us, "I won't be getting out of this bed again." He was right.

The boys were about to leave for a ski trip they had planned months before. At first, Don wanted them both to stay home; but as the drugs took effect, he changed his mind and told them he would be fine.

"You need to go on your trip," he told them.

That was a restless night for me. I spent the night checking on Don and giving him morphine every four hours so he wouldn't feel like he was suffocating. I awoke at six in the morning to him dialing the phone; it was on speaker because he couldn't hold it so I could hear everything. The first time it was a wrong number. He apologized and tried again.

"Jonathan… just wanted to make sure you're up and getting ready to head to the airport and catch your flight," I heard him say, followed by "I'm fine. You guys have a good time. I love you."

On New Year's Day, Don was calm, and his breathing wasn't labored because the morphine tricks the brain into thinking it has the oxygen it needs. I cooked black-eyed peas and corn bread that day to have for dinner, as I always did. I wanted to go on as normally as I could. Jaclyn and Brandy came over to spend the New Year with us and have black-eyed peas. When it was time for dinner, I went back to ask Don if he wanted something to eat.

"How about some black-eyed peas for good luck this year?" I asked.

"Don't think they're gonna help me this year, but you better have a big bowl of them," Don replied with a weak smile.

That night, he had a half of a peanut butter and jelly sandwich, and said that was the last thing he was going to eat. He was only eating to make us happy, but he couldn't anymore. Eating made it hurt to breathe because the muscles around his diaphragm were gone. So that was his last meal—peanut butter and jelly. He really had become more and more like the grandkids.

That night, some good friends stopped by to see Don. I held the wife back to explain what was going on, and when we walked into the bedroom, I saw Don holding his sheet up and wiping his eyes. Don had just told her husband that it was the last time he'd see him this side of heaven. We prayed and cried together that night.

The next day, Don called my mom, who is a retired hospice nurse.

"What is the process of dying?" he asked her. "What is going to happen to me and my body?" He wanted to know what to expect.

"I can't believe I'm having this conversation with my son-in-law who I adore," she said. She said she had to think of him as a patient while talking to him. When she hung up, she sobbed. So did I.

The next morning, the boys called from Colorado to check on Don. They called every day several times a day, just checking in and wanting to know if there were changes or if they needed to head home. It was a twelve-hour drive back home, so they knew they would need plenty of time.

"Are you sure we don't need to head back?" they asked again and again.

"You're fine," I'd insist. "I know what to watch for." I figured from the stories I had heard from other spouses of ALS patients that we had another week or two with Don.

Jennifer was headed in from Tulsa to stay the weekend. She wanted to help me out since the boys were gone and spend some time with her dad. Jaclyn also planned on spending the night. I was glad to have the girls there to help me get up through the night and help with Don every few hours. It was also just nice to have them there. It made it feel a little less scary to have my girls by my side.

Don took a nap that afternoon as I sewed baby bedding for our next grand baby. He woke up and started to call for me. "Lynda Sue!" he called out. When I went to him, I could see that he was confused.

"How long have I been in this chair?" he asked as he lay in his bed.

"Don, you're in your bed and you have just taken a two-hour nap," I told him.

He looked at the clock then back at me and said, "I think it's happening."

"I think so too."

"When Jennifer gets here, I want her to write my obituary," he told me.

I called Jennifer to prepare her. When she arrived, the first thing she did was check on Don.

"I'm here for the weekend, Dad," she said.

"I need you to do a few things," he told her, his mind clearer than it had been earlier. "I need you to write out my obit. It shouldn't take long. I really haven't done that much—"

Jen stopped him and said, "Dad, how about you give me just the key points, and I'll take care of it?"

"That sounds good, but before we do that, I need you to get on the computer and pay the ONG bill for Mom. I think the next few days are going to be busy for her, and I don't want her to have to worry about it," he replied. He was still getting things in order, taking care of me.

As I listened to Jen ask Don questions for his obituary, I knew it was painful for her. As a mother, my heart hurt for her. I walked into the room as she asked him the different boards he had been a member of.

"What was the title you held for MDA when you represented ALS?" she asked.

"I was the bull rider for them," he answered.

"What?" I interjected.

"I was the bull rider!" Don insisted.

I looked over at Jennifer, who was hiding her laughter behind a legal pad. We couldn't decide if he was joking or if he really thought he had been a bull rider. I looked at him and said, "Don Strahorn, you have never ridden a bull in your life."

He stared at me and said, "Well, fine, then put whatever you want!"

The CO_2 level was rising in his lungs, which meant he could not get deep enough breaths to clear his lungs, and that was causing confusion.

The boys called again shortly after that.

"Do we need to come home?"

"No, he's just a little confused," I told them.

That night before Jaclyn took the kids back to her house, each of the four grandkids went in to tell Don good-bye. Carter, Hutch, and Avery all climbed up in bed with their Papa, but Emily stayed planted at the end of his bed. The other three kissed him and told him they loved him. We asked Emily if she wanted to give Papa a kiss, but she just stood there at the end, pointed at him, and said, "You're going to heaven."

Later that evening, Bob came by to see Don. The last time he saw him, Don was struggling for air and frightened. When he walked into the room, the first thing he said was "Don, you look so beautiful and at peace." And he did. Don smiled, and they talked. There were smiles and tears throughout the conversation.

"I wish I could take you out on the golf course and beat you one more time," he said. They shared a laugh, and eventually, Bob left Don to rest.

Shortly after Bob left, Don started running a temperature. I called the hospice nurse to ask her what was going on; my first thought was pneumonia.

"It's probably dehydration," she told me. "Try some Tylenol." It was the only drug that we didn't have in our house, so the girls trekked out to get some. While the girls were gone, I sent the boys a message: "Come home."

Don became more confused throughout the night, but he was comfortable. I knew that we were coming to the end though. I started calling the boys constantly as the night progressed. They left Colorado just in front of a snowstorm to get back to Don. Every time I called, the boys held their breaths, afraid of what I was going to tell them as they made their way home. They were terrified they weren't going to make it, and because of that, they drove all night and stopped only twice in twelve hours for gas.

As the boys drove nonstop to get home, I called Don's mother, and all of us spent the night going in and out of Don's room checking on him and watching him. I never left his side. I stayed there, lying beside him and talking to him. I wanted to keep him from falling into a deep sleep. I was scared that if he did, he'd never open his eyes again. I rubbed his hands and head, telling him how much I loved him, telling him to hang on. At one point when I thought everyone else was asleep, I laid my head on the bed and began crying. I felt a hand rest on my back. It was Don.

"Lynda Sue, you are strong. You are so strong, and you can do this. You will never know how much I love you."

Jaclyn was awake when he said this to me, listening from the other room.

"I'm done," Don said suddenly. "I'm done." It was the middle of the night. The boys were still hours away.

"No, you're not!" I told him. "Just hang on, Don. The boys are almost here."

I kept getting updates on where the boys were: Colorado, Kansas, making the turn in Kansas headed for Oklahoma, just crossed the Oklahoma line, Stillwater, Guthrie…

"Don, just forty-five more minutes. They will be here in forty-five minutes. Just hang on."

They arrived at 9:30 a.m. on January 4. When they walked through the front door, you would've thought they were coming into a ski lodge. They looked like they were midmountainside on their skis when I called and had just hopped in the car and left. They went straight to their dad, sat beside him, and talked for about an hour.

"How was the trip?" Don asked, as if everything were normal for just a minute. He cracked a joke and told a couple of stories to lighten the mood, and then he told the boys he needed to rest.

That day, our house was like Grand Central Station. As the hospice nurse, friends, and family came and went, I made sure things were just as Don wanted them. He had made sure everything was in order for me; it was my time to make sure everything was in order for him. We had been preparing for this for seven years. I wanted to make sure his last days were as perfect as they could be. I put Christian music that he always listened on his iPod so it was playing in the background nonstop. We brought in chairs and surrounded his bed so we could all be close to him. He was home, with his family by his side. All Don ever wanted was to be at home when he passed away with his family there. And there we were.

As we surrounded Don, I could see the medication was working; he was not struggling to breath, but the CO_2 was building in his lungs. He was sleeping more and a little confused, but he was peaceful and surrounded by love. His best friend from childhood came in and told him he loved him and that he would watch over his family.

"Appreciate it," Don whispered. Those were the last words we could understand.

After that, Don was just waiting for Jesus. The hospice nurse came in at around four in the afternoon, put her hands on my shoulders, and said, "Lynda, I know you haven't slept at all."

"I'm not taking a nap!" I said, turning around to face her.

"No, I think we should just have everyone leave the room for just a little bit. We will move Don over some, and you can crawl up in bed with him and rest," she said.

Hospice is so wonderful. I do not know what I would've done without the amazing woman they sent to help us through those final moments and who was with us through the entire journey. Our nurse was more an angel; she became a dear friend that we trusted completely. And what she did that day was something I will never forget. She knew when I didn't know what I needed. I crawled in that bed for the last time and told Don how much I loved him.

"I am so proud of you," I told him. "I am so proud of how you've fought this. And I am thankful for the father and Papa you've been to our children and grandchildren." I stroked his hand as I said this. But this time, he didn't rub my head and back. He didn't talk to me about our life and our children; he was silent and still. "Thank you for loving me unconditionally," I said, and then I just lay there listening to him barely breathing and nuzzled into his chest for the last time. I felt his shallow breaths and heard his heart beating its final beats. That heart that beat for so many others was going to stop soon—that heart that had been given to me and our kids and grandkids and the church and so many others.

After about twenty minutes, Jennifer looked in to check on us and said, "Mom, have you looked at Daddy?"

"Yes," I told her, "go get your brothers and sister, grandmas, and Uncle Tom." Don was turning a light shade of blue from the lack of oxygen. It was coming. The CO_2 was taking over. There was no struggle or panic—no gasping or choking. He was just breathing shallow breaths and resting. All Don ever wanted was to be able to be at home when he passed away, have all his family with him, and for his CO_2 level to rise and take him peacefully. God was answering all those prayers.

"I think you should all climb up in that bed with him and talk to him, one last time," I said when all the kids were in the room. I watched our children one by one hug their father and whisper in his ear how much they loved him. I watched his mother tell her son that she didn't think she could go on living without him. His older brother sobbed and hugged him, all while he was slipping away. My mother, who just a few days earlier explained what and how this was all going to happen, cried like she was losing her own son. The nurse came back in to check on him. It was happening.

I sat down on the bed next to him, and everyone else stood there quietly crying. I held his beautiful face and said, "Go, Don. You can go now."

At 4:38 p.m., Don took two more breaths, and then he was gone. I had never heard such sincere sadness escape people in my life. The entire room began to wail. We cried as Don met the Lord. Our hearts broke as we sat there, a family suddenly missing a piece.

"This is not fair!" Jennifer sobbed as she fell over on Don.

I felt someone come up from behind me and grab me, sobbing. It was Jonathan. Ryan just sat there, his head in his hands, crying. My mom held Jaclyn, and Tom held his mom. We were all so broken. Everything ceased to make sense, and then the nurse confirmed it: he was gone. My Don was gone. His battle was over, but so was our life together. I'd have him only in memory now—only in my heart. I was an ALS widow.

"Dad's with Jesus now," Jaclyn said over all our tears.

Jonathan dried his eyes and said, "I can just see it now. Grandpa Jack is saying, 'Move over, Saint Peter. Here comes my son!'" And then we all broke out into laughter just picturing him walking into heaven and seeing his earthly and heavenly Fathers. Don left us laughing, like he always did.

Christmas 2013 2 weeks before Don passed away - Lynn (dad), Don, me, Jerry, Julie, Claudette (mom), Donna and Camille

Christmas eve 2013 Tom Poe and Brandon Clabes (Don's best friend since they were 7 years old)

Don and Jack (dad)

Christmas 2013 Don and me and all the grandkids - Carter,
Carlie, Hutch, Don, Avery, me, Cooper, Harison and Emily

FINAL WORDS

The greatest honor of my life was caring for Don. I have to admit that on some days, it was hard and I was tired and my body and mind were so weak that I would have to remind myself that I wasn't doing this just for him but that I was also serving Jesus. I would go back and relive every moment with him again and again. All the pain that ALS brought will never overshadow the love that Don put into this world. He fought the good fight, and he did with a light heart and a smile on his face.